THE FINANCIAL ADVISORY

THE FINANCIAL ADVISORY

Hundreds of Ways to Save and Invest Your Money

MILTON PIERCE

A PERIGEE BOOK

Perigee Books
are published by
The Putnam Publishing Group
200 Madison Avenue
New York, NY 10016

Published simultaneously in Canada by
General Publishing Co. Limited, Toronto

Library of Congress Cataloging in Publication Data

Pierce, Milton.
The financial advisory.

1. Finance, Personal. I. Title.
HG179.P54 1984 332.024 84-14796
ISBN 0-399-50983-6

Printed in the United States of America

1 2 3 4 5 6 7 8 9 10

CONTENTS

A book of this magnitude is never the work of one lone individual. I would like to offer my sincere thanks to Kathy Chase Johnson, Scott Leventhal, and Judy Newman, who helped. Most of all, I would like to express my gratitude to the lady who makes it all possible, Mrs. Deborah Pierce.

INTRODUCTION

This book can save you a lot of money.

Buying a used car? Preparing your taxes? Investing in a new home? *The Financial Advisory* can show you a few tricks that will help you to save a bundle. You'll find advice on how to avoid a few common (and uncommon) pitfalls in buying a used car, tax deductions you may have overlooked (or didn't realized existed at all), and some of the things to watch for in buying or selling a house. In fact, *The Financial Advisory* offers a wealth of information and advice on how to save money and how to invest it.

The first part of this book offers suggestions on how to cut down on unnecessary expenditures in your personal life, how to save on medical expenses, how to save money on buying and maintaining a car, how to reduce those education expenses for your college-bound children, and things to keep in mind when shopping by mail—including how to get your money back if you're not satisfied with the product. There is also information on ways to cut vacation expenses (suggestions my own family has tested and proved while having a truly marvelous holiday), and tax information which can save you dollars *now*.

The second part of this book concentrates on investments which can help you to *increase* your savings and build on your financial security. There are explanations and tips on stocks, mutual funds, bonds, whether to use a broker or not, and how to complain when you feel your broker is not doing enough. There are also tips on investing in precious metals, diamonds and other gems, and the advantages to collecting stamps, coins, artwork, and many other rare objects as investment properties.

This is not a book based on abstract theory however; it is a book forged out of a lifetime of experience in the financial world. Many of the suggestions, tips, and hints in this book arise out of personal experience. When I discuss the advantages of owning a second home, for example, it is because the Pierce family has that second home. When I suggest how to complain to a retailer about faulty products, it is because my wife Debbie is probably the world's champion complainer in those situations. I think the experience factor will prove an added plus that most financial primers cannot offer.

I do have one request of you as you read through *The Financial Advisory*. Do you have a money-saving idea or trick that you've discovered? Why not write to me—personally—so that I can include your idea in the next edition of this book (of course I will give you credit). You'll have the pleasure of knowing your suggestion will help many other people. Here's how you can reach me:

Milton Pierce
c/o Perigee Books
200 Madison Avenue
New York, NY 10016

Happy—and profitable—reading.

THE FINANCIAL ADVISORY

Part One

PERSONAL PLANNING

I.
YOUR HOME

If you've ever been besieged by bill collectors, had to face unexpected expenses, or hoped to make a major investment in a home or a new car, you've probably said, "I wish I had planned for this."

This section will provide basic information about personal expenses and home expenditures, guidelines on insurance and taxes, special information that will help you use your credit cards more efficiently, and tips on shopping by mail, warranties, cutting educational costs, and enjoying a cheaper vacation. In other words, the things you need to know about coping with the complexities of daily life.

HOMEOWNING

A home is probably the most important investment you will make, the one that is certain to rise in value over the years. For those of you who are contemplating buying a home in the future, high interest rates and a stagnant housing market can hurt you.

You may wonder if you'll be able to afford that dream house.

The advantages of owning a home are numerous. Yet many of you who want to leave apartment living are finding it difficult to find an affordable house. The following pages will show you some imaginative things that people are doing to buy homes despite the high interest rates, including how you can cut your expenses once you get a home, and how to spot the rip-off artists who prey on homeowners.

A LITTLE-KNOWN TRICK THAT CAN SAVE BIG MONEY IN HOME BUYING

Have you ever considered buying a home, only to be frightened off by the high cost? Well, a new trend has started in home buying to help overcome the high cost of buying a house: joint purchasing. Young couples just beginning their careers sometimes find this to be an extremely advantageous way to buy their first house. What is needed is a two-family unit or an older, larger house that can be separated into two living quarters. Although you will undoubtedly lose some privacy, mortgages, downpayments, and utility bills can be split down the middle, making an impossibly expensive proposition suddenly affordable. Here are 5 things to keep in mind:

1. *Legal Implications.* After teaming up with another couple, find a lawyer who is familiar with "tenants in common" agreements. Every legal possibility, no matter how remote, must be covered: divorce, death, catastrophic illness are a few. Could you lose your share of the property if a judgment is filed against your "partner"? If you choose to sell, how much say should the other couple have in approving the new tenants? If you are on good

terms with your partners, simple negotiation should resolve any such conflict.

2. *Zoning Laws.* Make sure you understand the zoning laws of the city you purchase a home in. Some couples have ended up in court after making additions to their home because such additions were technically in violation of local ordinances.

3. *Obtaining a Mortgage.* You should not have trouble getting financing for your home. Many banks feel more confident having four incomes and four signatures instead of two. You should receive the live-in mortgage rate, as opposed to the rate investors in most partnerships are charged.

4. *Looking Ahead.* After two or more years of ownership, you may consider turning your house into a cooperative. Transferring ownership to a corporation will make it much easier for any new buyer to receive co-op financing. Your tax deductions will not change, and you will be able to borrow money against the shares if necessary.

5. *Lifestyles.* One cautionary note: Before deciding on joint-purchasing a home, make sure that you and the other couple have similar career and lifestyle objectives. You can imagine what it would be like if it was discovered later that one couple hated children and the other wanted to have five.

6 WAYS THE HOUSING CRUNCH AFFECTS THE ECONOMY—AND YOU

Buying a home used to be the dream of every young couple in America. As recently as 1970, according to U.S. Government statistics, half the people in this country could have afforded a median-priced home (then $23,400). Today, only 10 percent can afford to buy a house, based on the standard rule that they spend no more than 23 percent of their taxable income on mortgage payments. Of those who do buy, 50 percent ignore the aforementioned rule. Here are 6 ways the problem affects you:

1. *Overextension.* Many people who really shouldn't buy a house do—with family help, largely as a buffer against further inflation. These people are becoming "house poor." Although they have a house, many can't afford to furnish it, decorate it, or improve it. What's more, many of them can't afford consumer goods and services, a spillover which affects merchants.

2. *Apartment Living.* Those who can't afford homes usually live in an apartment. The demand, especially in the more crowded cities, has encouraged landlords to screen prospective tenants and refuse rentals to those with modest incomes. Those who want two bedrooms end up with one; those who want one end up with a studio. Often you have to forget the rule of not spending more than a quarter of your pretax income on rent: it just doesn't hold water anymore for many people.

3. *Rent Controls.* Rent controls, used in many cities to protect apartment dwellers, have discouraged new building. Although rents on newly leased apartments have soared, the prices of controlled apartments have remained artificially low. So low, in fact, that many developers are turning their buildings into co-ops or condominiums in return for a quick profit. In the period from 1980 to 1984, the number of apartments converted and sold more than doubled. That figure will continue to rise, especially in major cities like New York and Los Angeles, where the demand is greatest.

4. *Sellers.* The crunch in housing is by no means restricted to the buyer. A seller may price himself out of the market by asking too much, or he or she can sell too quickly and get a better offer just a few days after the close. The seller, of course, has one distinct advantage: he's not buying.

5. *Mortgage Rates.* Lending institutions, most of whom supply

mortgages, are financially strapped. Savers who provide the money the banks lend are withdrawing because of low interest rates and better returns on money market funds, IRA's, etc. And, say the banks, low mortgage ceilings in certain states make it more profitable to lend the money elsewhere, particularly in states with high ceilings.

6. *Housing Starts.* The cost of land, labor, and materials has been rising steadily. Many builders are afraid of huge cost overruns. Government regulations, largely those at the local level, can add as much as 20 percent to the cost of a new home. The government estimates it now takes much longer (three or four times) for a builder to move from the planning stage into construction.

With the upswing in the economy, the demand for housing is high. Prices are expected to rise faster than salaries, putting even two-income families into a large financial hole. Many experts agree that the days of finding a dream house are over, and Americans are going to have to accept less for more.

HOW TO SPOT RIP-OFFS IN THE HOME IMPROVEMENT GAME

You say you need a home improvement? An expanded driveway, aluminum siding, a new kitchen? Sounds simple—find a contractor, get the work done. But it's not that easy. There are many unscrupulous home improvement people, and you should be aware of them and their bag of tricks. Here are 5 common swindles:

1. *"Bait and Switch."* This is an old gimmick, but people still get caught. An advertisement offers a great product at an unbelievably low price. When the salesman shows up, though,

he degrades the advertised bargain and tries to switch you to something that's much more expensive. That's the bait and switch.

2. *Resurfacing Driveways.* These roving rip-off artists knock on your door and tell you they just happen to be in the neighborhood. They've got some leftover materials, and if you like, they'll finish your driveway at an incredibly low price. Be careful. They'll do a bad job or none at all.

3. *Roofing and Siding Games.* A "contractor" rings your bell and shows you some loose shingles which he says fell from your roof. Fix it, he warns, or your roof will cave in, probably tomorrow. Don't shell out a nickel. You'll probably end up with a lousy roof or none at all.

A typical siding game is a "chain referral." A siding (or carpeting) salesman will offer you a terrific bargain on the product if you allow your home to be used as a "model" for other potential customers. Unsuspectingly, you sign such an agreement. Unfortunately, it's an iron-clad contract that says you have agreed to pay (usually an exorbitant fee) for the product.

4. *"Crew Switching."* Two groups selling the same product work different parts of the neighborhood. Their prices are outrageous, and they almost always get turned down. The trick? They switch territories, offering lower (but still high) prices than the first crew mentioned. You, of course, have no idea that the crews are working together to rip you off.

5. *"You Have Termites."* A swindler says that termites were found in the neighborhood. He says he'll inspect your house for free, and returns with a jar full of—what else?

Don't Get Burned. If you need something done, seek out a professional who has a good reputation in your area. If someone you think is a con artist rings your bell, let the Better Business Bureau and the police know about it. And don't ever sign anything unless you know exactly what you're getting.

10 WAYS TO CUT YOUR UTILITY COSTS

If you are a homeowner or apartment dweller paying for utilities, you know that they can be one of your largest expenses. In this day and age of soaring energy costs, here are 10 ways you can save money:

1. *Reduce Heating Costs.* Well-insulated walls and ceilings, storm windows and doors, and weather-stripping for window frames and doors can stop the escape of heat from your home. The government is offering energy tax credits for expenditures like these, so they may prove to be a valuable long-term investment.

2. *Increase the Efficiency of Your Heating Unit.* Have a serviceman clean, adjust, and tune your gas furnace once every three years. You need to do the same to an oil burner, but more frequently, at least once a year. Dirty air filters can also cause problems, so they should be cleaned or replaced every few months.

3. *Adjust Your Thermostat.* By turning your thermostat down at bedtime or when you aren't at home, you can save money. If you need it set at 75 or higher, it's a signal that your home is poorly insulated.

4. *Switch to Gas.* Electric water heaters, stoves, and clothes dryers are the most expensive appliances to operate. You should consider switching to gas models unless the cost of natural gas is prohibitive in your area. There are a few places, however, where electricity is cheaper than natural gas. Your local utilities can provide information about rates for each.

5. *Operate Appliances at Full Capacity.* It may be more convenient to run a washing machine, clothes dryer or dishwasher when you don't have a full load, but you're wasting money. Use these appliances when you have enough laundry or dirty dishes for a full load. Don't take this practice to excess by

overloading, however, because you'll endanger the life of the product.

6. *Use Energy Efficiently in the Kitchen.* Make sure burners and ovens are turned off after use. Flat-bottomed, straight-sided pans distribute the heat more evenly than other pans. Avoid overcooking by boiling slowly and gradually. A slow boil will cook as quickly as a rapid one. Avoid constantly opening the oven while food is being prepared. Valuable heat can escape.

7. *Take Care of Your Refrigerator.* Defrost your freezer regularly. Your refrigerator will not operate as efficiently if it has to contend with thick frost. The rear cooling pipes should be kept dust free. Check door gaskets and replace them regularly.

8. *Purchase Efficient Appliances.* Appliances manufactured by different companies use varying amounts of energy. The power ratings, found on the machine or in the operating instructions, will give you an idea of its energy efficiency.

9. *Air Conditioning.* More Americans have central air conditioning or room air conditioners than ever before. Your utility bills can be staggering during the summer months, but there are some things you can do about it. Draw shades and blinds when the cooling system is in use, don't run the air conditioner if you aren't home, limit air conditioning to one or two rooms, and insulate your attic.

10. *Water Bills.* Dripping faucets and leaking toilet tanks are the biggest villains when it comes to high water bills. You can probably make minor repairs such as these without calling a plumber. A more efficient shower head, which you can get at a hardware store, can also save you money.

Most of these items seem small when compared to your energy consumption. Some of them are, but a simple act like closing windows when the air conditioning is on can save energy and money.

PREPARING TO SELL YOUR HOUSE

Your home is probably the largest investment you have, so when you're ready to sell, you want to make sure you get the best price you can. Here are 6 things to consider when you attempt to sell:

1. *Pricing.* Putting the proper price tag on your home can be a difficult job. If the price is too high, you may discourage prospective buyers. If it is too low, a "something must be wrong with this house" stigma may be attached.

- Determine what the market will bear. If any homes in your neighborhood were sold recently, find out for how much.
- Find out what new homes in your area are selling for.
- If your house was recently assessed for tax purposes, that figure may be a good guide. If not, a real estate appraiser will assess it for a fee.
- Set the price 10 to 15 percent above the appraisal. It will keep away those people who are "always looking," but you may just find a buyer who is willing to pay that price. In any case, it will give you some margin to play with if you have to come down on the price.

2. *Repairs.* Make your house as desirable as possible. Fix any broken windows, cracked steps, or leaky faucets. You might consider painting the exterior or just touching it up a bit. Avoid major interior repairs like painting, since everybody has their own tastes.

3. *Advertising.* Where you advertise depends largely on where you expect to get prospective buyers from. If your house is very expensive, you could advertise in professional journals or business publications. But a local suburban newspaper should have low classified rates, so it would probably be the best buy for the money.

4. *List the House's Benefits.* You should prepare a fact sheet for interested buyers to look at. Include such things as the size of the lot, the taxes, number of rooms, and its proximity to shopping and schools. List advantages that might not be obvious to the naked eye such as central air conditioning, a new water heater, or an electric garage door opener.

Items like these increase the value of your house, so make sure prospective buyers know about them.

5. *Negotiating Price.* This of course is entirely up to you. If you get what you're asking for, by all means take it. If you have to come down in price, remember that you won't really lose anything, since you jacked up the price to begin with.

6. *Should You Get a Broker?* If you're willing to show the house and place the ads, why pay a broker? If, however, you have a tough time finding buyers, then get a broker.

BEING A LANDLORD CAN BE PROFITABLE

Many people are discovering the advantages of owning and renting apartments. All it takes is some patience on your part and a willingness to wait for the right opportunity. Here are 8 things you should keep in mind if you are looking for a building to rent:

1. People who sell property do so because they need the money. The faster they need it, the lower the price will be.

2. Be careful of buying buildings in large cities. Decaying neighborhoods and rent controls are just two of the reasons it is wiser to look for properties in small towns or suburbs.

3. Two-bedroom units are the easiest to rent because there are many families who just can't afford to purchase a home.

4. Look for properties that will appreciate in value. That means the neighborhood should be good; the other homes well taken

care of. In other words, there should be numerous advantages to the prospective renter.

5. Purchase a building you can improve. The improvements don't have to be major, but you can substantially increase the value of a property just by adding a fresh coat of paint.

6. Find out how often the property has been sold in the recent past. A building that has changed hands a number of times may not be as profitable as one that hasn't.

7. Scrutinize the inside of the building. Leaks and other internal improvements can hurt your chances for a good profit.

8. Get advice on room arrangements, the best types of floor and wall coverings, and ways to cut energy costs. Any improvements you can make, especially those which you can do yourself, will increase the value of the property.

2.
INSURANCE

9 WAYS TO MAKE YOUR INSURANCE DOLLARS WORK BETTER FOR YOU

Today's new risks make insurance coverage more important than ever. Juries are awarding larger and larger sums in liability cases. Executives can be held responsible in product liability cases or for mismanagement of pension funds.

Here are 9 ways you can save yourself huge insurance problems later on:

1. *Raise Your Auto Liability Coverage.* With juries awarding record sums in liability suits, you must make an effort to protect yourself fully with auto insurance, especially if you earn $50,000 or more a year. Coverage of $300,000 to $500,000 sounds like a large amount, but it really isn't. The difference in premiums is small, and shopping around can save you another 25 percent. Obviously, the easiest way of keeping your premiums down is to have a good driving record.

2. *Have Your Home Appraised.* You will probably be surprised to find that your home is dangerously underinsured. Get a current appraisal and bring your coverage to 85 or 90 percent of the

replacement cost. This is an important point—the amount of coverage should reflect what it would cost to replace the house in *today's market.* It will also ensure that your possessions are adequately covered. An inflation rider is available in some states; you should increase your coverage 8 to 10 percent every year. This increased coverage is usually around $100 for each $10,000 of additional coverage.

3. *Get a Personal Property Floater.* Replacement costs of valuables such as furs, jewelry, and antiques are up, meaning your coverage may not be enough. If your homeowner's coverage has a strict limit, $500 for example, on the replacement cost of such items, you may be in for some headaches. You can purchase floater coverage on specific items that insures everything but normal wear and tear. The cost is not high and varies according to the worth of the object covered.

4. *Consider an Umbrella Policy.* Since liability coverage in auto and homeowner's insurance is too low, an umbrella policy can insure you against any type of liability claim up to $5 million. It does not cover business-related risks, just personal cases. The cost is minimal, generally $100 for each $1 million of coverage.

5. *If You Are a Business Executive, Consider Directors and Officers Coverage.* With the number of government and class-action suits filed against businesses growing rapidly, most executives who could be considered liable do not have such coverage. Although most large concerns offer such coverage, many medium and smaller sized businesses do not. Company officers can only urge their employer to cover them (since they cannot buy it individually), but outside directors can cover themselves for $5 million. The cost is high—over $600 per $1 million of coverage—but so is the risk.

6. *Supplement Your Disability Coverage.* Although most companies offer their employees disability coverage at little or no cost, many of these plans contain large gaps for more recent

workers. With the cost of living increasing, it is a wise move to get some private disability coverage. A supplemental policy will pay 40 to 50 percent of your salary to age 65. You can save 10 percent by shopping around, and the cost is reflected by the monthly benefits you would receive.

7. *And Your Major Medical.* Major medical is offered by most companies, but many have strict limits on the total they will pay out. With hospital costs going up, you should consider raising your coverage to more than $100,000, depending on the amount you would receive from your employer. The cost is around $800 per year for a family of four.

8. *Increase Your Term Insurance.* This relatively cheap form of insurance is good if you have children to educate or a mortgage to pay. For young people, the costs are minimal, and a large increase in premiums doesn't occur until after your forty-eighth birthday. By that time you will probably no longer need the coverage. For the best price break, buy $50,000 or more, and shop around since prices vary.

9. *Consider More Life Insurance.* Ordinary life insurance builds up cash value. This type of policy is more expensive than term insurance, but the cash value of the policy increases and you can draw on it at age sixty-five, when your need for insurance is not as great as in your middle years. You may also consider combining your term and life policies into one contract. The premiums will be less, but the coverage will be virtually the same.

These points can help you determine the sufficiency of your insurance coverage in the face of rising inflation. Don't be afraid to shop around and take out a policy with the company that offers the best deal.

HOW TO CHOOSE LIFE INSURANCE THAT'S RIGHT FOR YOU

Life insurance is important. Even though most of us realize that, many of us have the wrong type of coverage. Here are 4 different kinds of life insurance and the persons they are best suited for:

1. *Term Insurance.* This is the cheapest type of coverage, usually good for young people whose incomes will increase in later years. The policy covers you for a specific period of time and will pay off only if you die during that period. It is good to have as a stopgap until you can afford straight life. Try to get a convertible or renewable policy. Decreasing term might be acceptable if you are paying off a large debt, like a mortgage or a loan on your education.

2. *Straight Life.* This is the most common type of insurance. The premiums are higher, but they offer permanent protection. In addition, the cost of the policy doesn't increase with age and you can borrow against the value of the policy.

3. *Limited-payment Life.* A spin-off of straight life, you pay higher premiums over a shorter period of time. The advantage is that the policy builds up cash value quicker than straight life. Good for people whose incomes are concentrated over a short period of time.

4. *Endowment.* This is a policy that stresses savings for a particular purpose such as a child's education or paying off a home. Because of the emphasis on savings, the policy builds up cash value rapidly. It is expensive.

Choosing a Policy. There is really no way to tell you exactly what type of coverage is best. You should, however, consider your income, the amount of money you have saved, and anticipated future expenses like your mortgage or the children's education.

Choosing a Company. Best's Insurance Guide, available in most libraries and bookstores, is probably the most helpful tool in choosing an insurance company. It rates every company relative to its financial stability. Don't limit yourself. Talk to about one-fourth of the companies available to you and see which offers the best deal.

INSURING AGAINST INFLATION

Stolen-property values boom with inflation. Unfortunately, some insurance policies covering theft in the home or business are not in step with inflation. Companies have liberalized their limitations by increasing the premiums, but many categories still do not exceed $1000.

One alternative is "floater" insurance to protect against the loss of valuables. In these policies you can set the value of each item, based on the bill of sale and appraisal. A drawback is that insurance companies have the option to replace the property stolen at the current market value, which in some cases may be much less than what was originally paid. On the plus side, floaters avoid depreciation and cover loss in the case of mysterious disappearance. However, the policyholder is responsible for the amount of coverage he or she wishes to carry.

Items not covered by a floater policy, such as clothing and appliances, are goods that depreciate rapidly. You can protect these possessions and keep up with inflation by looking into a replacement-value policy. In these policies, reimbursement may be limited to four times the depreciated cost of the item.

So check your present policy and be sure you are protected against today's inflation and today's thieves.

3.
YOUR CAR

It used to cost me $7 to fill the gas tank of my compact car. It now costs more than double that. Every time I pull into the gas station it seems prices have gone up another penny or two.

And yet gasoline isn't the only increasing expense in driving a car. The cost of owning a new car goes up every year, forcing more and more people to hold on to their automobiles longer than in the past. To put this in a more positive light, that fact is forcing people to take better care of the cars they already own.

This chapter will offer valuable suggestions you can use in looking for a new car, purchasing tires, spotting a dishonest car dealer, or choosing a mechanic.

---

10 WAYS TO GET THE BEST DEAL ON A NEW CAR

Although car prices today are very high, rebates, discounts on options, and other such incentives can be used to your advantage.

But you must know what you want. Here are 10 tips worth considering:

1. *Know What You Want.* A new-car buying guide can be extremely helpful in allowing you to determine, to a great extent, the dealer's price before markup. These guides, available at newsstands and in bookstores, list every make and model available. Use this method to find the car that will best fit your needs before you get stuck with something you'll be unhappy with.

2. *Determine Your Bargaining Power.* The difference between the base cost (what the dealer pays for the car) and the suggested list price will give you a general idea of how much you can haggle with the dealer. The markups on most cars are well over 10 percent, but many dealers are willing to settle for less.

3. *Don't Be Talked Into Unwanted Options.* Many dealers make their money on options, the little extras that make a car more attractive, but may be, for practical purposes, useless. Items such as power windows may be convenient, but they are harder to fix should something go wrong. Watch out for extras such as rustproofing or undercoating. They are probably worthless unless you plan to own the car for a long time.

4. *Get Current Information.* Because the standard buying guides are printed soon after the new-model year begins, they may not have up-to-date information on rebates or price increases. Car/Puter International Corporation, 1603 Bushwick Ave., Brooklyn, NY (1-800-221-4001 or 718-455-2500) will send you up-to-date computer printouts on any new car. You will receive information regarding the dealer's cost, the suggested retail price, a complete list of available options, and notification of rebates, special sales, and freight charges in your area. You will also receive the name of a specific dealer who will take your order for $75 above cost. This printout is $15, refundable if you purchase from the dealer. It's available by phone.

5. *Play Dumb in the Showroom.* Don't let the salesman know

what you're thinking until you feel comfortable with him. Even if you already have a specific model and price in mind, let him try to talk to you about other ideas.

6. *Beware of "I'll Have to Get the Manager's Okay."* A much used ploy by a salesman who sees a big commission slipping out of his grasp, it is designed to force your hand—"take it or leave it." Unless your demands are extremely unreasonable, no dealer will let you walk out the door when he's that close to making a sale.

7. *Check the Dealer's Record on Service.* The reliability of a dealer's service department should be a consideration. If you're spending $10,000 on a new car, you should expect efficient service if something goes wrong, especially during the initial warranty period, when rattles and other problems may develop. That being the case, it might be advisable to spend a little more money and buy a car from a dealer who has a reputation for prompt and efficient service.

8. *Shop Around.* Most dealers expect you to get a number of prices for the car you want. If they claim they will "beat any deal," don't come to them with an outlandish, fabricated figure. They'll see right through it. Many dealers will drop their "final price," however, rather than lose a sale.

9. *Don't Settle for Less—Or More.* Stick to your guns. Don't accept something "off the floor" that has a few more things than you want or need. If a dealer is offering something like that, there must be a reason for it. Expect to wait for delivery, and don't allow the chance to "get it today" to cloud your judgment.

10. *Remember That the Purchase Isn't Over When the Order Is Made.* When the car comes in, double and triple check your list to make sure there are no "hidden extras." Look for chips, scratches, or things like missing dome lights and faded carpets. You are not obligated to take the car if it isn't exactly what you

ordered. If that is the case, the dealer may drop the price even more just to get the car off the lot.

HOW TO SAVE MONEY ON A CAR RENTAL

Prices for rental cars vary widely. By comparison shopping, you can save money. Here are 8 general rules to follow:

1. Try to figure out in advance how many miles you expect to drive on your trip. Include contingencies such as getting lost, unexpected side trips, and detours caused by bad weather conditions or roadwork. If the trip will be a long one, get the lowest per-mile charge you can.
2. Estimate how many days you will need the car. You may do better with a weekly rate than a daily one.
3. Choose the type of car you need carefully. A big car will cost you more in gas money and in rental fees than a compact.
4. Sacrificing convenience may save you money. A rental agency at the airport may charge more than one that is down the road a bit. Some inconveniently located agents offer things like shuttle buses to and from the airport.
5. Inquire about special deals like weekend rates; some of these plans offer unlimited mileage.
6. Check out the car before you drive away. Otherwise you could be charged for damages present before you used it.
7. If you won't be returning the car to the same city, find out if there is a drop-off charge and what it is. You can usually find an agent who won't charge this fee.
8. When comparison shopping, figure out the "per-day costs" of the rental. Include in that cost the rental charge, the mileage fee, and what you expect to pay for gasoline. The one that offers the cheapest per-day costs is the one for you.

HOW TO SAVE MONEY ON TIRES

Your tires are probably one of the most important parts of your car. They are expensive, but by shopping around, you can usually get a good deal on tires that are right for you.

1. Find a reputable dealer. Your best bet is to talk to friends and find out where they purchase tires. Franchised dealers of nationally advertised brands, established service stations, and large retailers will probably offer the best deal.
2. Compare prices and look for sales. The best months for purchasing tires are May and August.
3. Find out what the price includes. Are mounting and balancing extra? What type of warranty do you get?
4. Watch out for fictitious price reductions.
5. Beware of far-out claims.
6. The load capacity for the four tires should be equal to the weight of your car with a full load. This is a federal standard and more helpful than the number of plies.
7. Do not mix and match tires. If you want radial tires, then get four. If that isn't possible, then at least have the same tires on one axle.
8. If you want to buy retreads, make sure you know who does the job for the dealer. A reputable retreading firm will inspect their tires before sending them out to the dealer.

Source: *Sylvia Porter's Money Book,* Vol. I, p. 378

20 WAYS TO MAKE SURE YOU'RE GETTING A GOOD USED CAR

There's nothing wrong with buying a used car except that you don't know how "used" it is. Here are 20 things you can check to make sure the used car you purchase won't die after a few months of driving.

1. Go during the day so you can inspect the interior of the car. A car that's worn on the inside is an indication of trouble ahead. A heavily worn brake is a sign the odometer may have been tampered with.

2. Check the tires for wear. If they are new or badly worn, it's an indication the car has more than 40,000 miles on it. If the tires are unevenly worn, it might mean the front end needs an alignment job, or the brakes or shocks are bad.

3. Check rust spots to see if they've gone through the metal.

4. Check the paint job. Any change in color means the car was probably in a serious accident. That means trouble.

5. Roll down all of the windows, open and close the doors, trunk and hood. If any are tough to open, the car needs repairs.

6. Shake each front tire hard. A flexible tire or noises could indicate loose ball joints or a worn suspension.

7. Depress the brake steadily. If it goes down slowly, there may be a leak in the brake system.

8. Start the engine and listen for any suspicious noises. If the car idles rough, the dealer might be disguising a bad engine.

9. Check the electrical system including windshield wipers, lights, turn signals, heater, etc.

10. Check the shock absorbers by pushing down the fender at one corner. If the car bounces for more than a few seconds, it might be worn.

11. Kneel behind the center of the car and ask the salesman to drive away. If the car moves down the street at an angle, it might have been in a major accident.

12. See how smoothly the car accelerates.

13. Drive up a steep hill to make sure the gears don't slip.

14. Drive forward and backward a few times to check the transmission.

15. Check the brakes by accelerating to 45 on a straight road with no traffic. Step hard on the brake and make sure it stops smooth and straight, without pulling.

16. Make some left and right turns to see how it handles. The wheel shouldn't be loose, but it shouldn't be difficult to turn either.

17. Drive down a long hill and take your foot off the gas. Before you reach the bottom, accelerate and see what comes out of the exhaust pipe. If the smoke is blue, you've got a bad engine.

18. Drive on a bumpy road. If there are shakes and rattles, you have trouble steering and the car jumps over bumps, the suspension system might be gone.

19. Check for overheating and leaky hoses. Keep an eye on the temperature gauge while driving.

20. Drive more than 2 or 3 miles. A short ride can mask a bad engine.

Even after you check these things yourself, let your mechanic inspect the car thoroughly. He'll be able to tell you if you're buying someone else's problems.

WHAT IT COSTS TO RUN YOUR CAR

If you knew how much it cost you to operate your car, you might take up hitchhiking. The Hertz Corporation completed a study showing how much it costs to run your car per mile in ten U.S. cities. The cost per mile includes gasoline and service station costs; maintenance, including parts and repairs; registration and insurance fees; loan interest and depreciation. The figures do not include parking expenses or tolls since each area is different. Although the cost per mile has gone up with new car prices and insurance rates, this will give you some comparison of how much it costs to run a car in your area:

City	Cost Per Mile (for compact cars)
Los Angeles	40.1
New York	38.2
San Francisco	37.5
Miami	37.2
Chicago	36.3
Denver	37.1
Houston	36.8
San Diego	36.1
Washington	35.2
Dallas	35.1
National Average	34.5

Even according to the National Average figures, it is costing you about $4 every ten miles you drive. Shocking? Read on, and see how you can reduce those expenses.

---

10 WAYS TO GET MORE MILES PER GALLON

With a gallon of gasoline approaching the $1.50 mark in some places, the Federal Government and private companies are attempting to teach consumers new driving methods designed to get higher gas mileage. These techniques won't turn your gas guzzler into a penny pincher, but they will save you money over the long haul.

The program, known as the National Energy Efficient Driving System, grew out of the Arab oil embargo of 1973, when American consumers first experienced higher prices and long lines at the pumps. The 10 techniques can be easily conquered by any driver. They involve not just physical skills, but thinking behind the wheel as well. Dr. John Eberhard, of the United States Department of Transportation, says, "We found we could train people to be more fuel efficient in just a 45-minute question-and-answer session."

1. Get the car to cruising speed as quickly as possible. Acceleration, either fast or slow, uses much more fuel than driving at a constant rate of speed.

2. After a comfortable speed has been reached, ease up on the accelerator without decelerating. It's called "soft-pedaling," and it can gain you two to three miles per gallon.

3. Riding the brake can also waste fuel. Suggestion: Don't brake unnecessarily. On the highway, stay three seconds (about 75 yards) behind the car in front, using engine drag and air friction instead of the brake whenever traffic slows up.

4. Learn to anticipate traffic lights and coast through when green. Allow momentum, not fuel, to carry you up to a toll plaza.

5. If your car is air conditioned, use it. It takes more gas to overcome the air draft of open windows than to run the cooling system.

6. Keep tires properly inflated, according to the owner's manual.

7. Empty the trunk as much as possible. The extra weight will show up at the pumps.

8. Do not let a car idle for more than one minute.

9. Avoid stop-and-go driving by maintaining a steady pace, regardless of the speed.

10. Do not exceed the 55-mile-an-hour speed limit. It only increases the wind resistance and won't save you that much time.

It will take some diligence to learn and perfect these methods, but experts insist the average driver can increase his or her fuel efficiency by 30 percent a gallon by using these techniques, a savings of 200 gallons every year.

---

10 RULES FOR SAVING MONEY WHEN CHOOSING AN AUTO MECHANIC

When something goes wrong with your car, you want to be sure it will be fixed promptly and correctly. Here are 10 rules you should follow to avoid getting taken for a ride:

1. Have a general idea where you would take the car if something happened today.
2. If you can find a good mechanic, stick with him or her for all types of repairs. The more he or she knows about your car and your driving habits, the better off you'll be.
3. Understand the options open to you: a new car dealer, a service station, or a shop which specializes in transmissions, alignments, brake jobs, or other types of repairs.
4. Go to a mechanic who is a member of the Better Business Bureau or an independent trade group. If your state licenses mechanics, that's even better.
5. If you can't speak directly with the mechanic who will work on your car, find another shop.
6. Look for a shop which wants your repeat business and gives you a careful diagnosis of the problem. A mechanic who lets you tell what the problem is doesn't care about you.
7. Stick with places that will give you a detailed, written estimate of the work involved.
8. If it's possible, schedule your work in advance and get it done during the middle of the week.
9. Be specific about the work you want done. What's a tune-

up to one mechanic may be something totally different to another.

10. Take a course in do-it-yourself auto repair. Even if you never repair your own car, you'll be better able to judge another mechanic's work.

HOW TO SPOT AUTO REPAIR RIP-OFFS

You're on a trip, far from home, and something goes wrong with your car. You pull into a service station and find out your engine has to be overhauled. Watch out! You could become a victim of one of the biggest rip-offs in America today. Here are 5 tricks used by unscrupulous mechanics who prey on unsuspecting out-of-towners:

1. Your tires might get slashed while you aren't looking. "Gee, you've got a slow leak. You better buy a new tire."

2. The mechanic shows you a dipstick with dirty oil, "proof" you need an oil change or a new filter. All motor oil gets "dirty" after it circulates in the engine.

3. The attendant drains your battery acid, replaces it with regular water and says you have a dead battery. Baking soda can be put in a battery to make it appear dead, also.

4. A hose can easily be punctured while the mechanic is checking under the hood.

5. Bending alternator wires to make alternator lights go on (signaling trouble in the charging system).

The best protection you have is to get your car tuned before you leave on a trip. Have your tires checked, your oil changed, and check the fan belt, the battery, and the hoses. If you do encounter a problem on the road, keep an eye on the attendant when he's checking the car. Read your credit card receipt to make sure the amount was totaled. If not, charges could be added even though you signed the bill.

4.
HIGHER EDUCATION
Ways of Cutting Costs

Will you be able to pay for your children's higher education when they're ready? That's a question many of us are asking as tuition zooms upward. The pages to follow will tell you how to give your children a tax-free education, which universities cost the most, and how you can take advantage of college scholarships and grants.

HOW TO PUT YOUR SON OR DAUGHTER THROUGH COLLEGE WITH A MINIMUM OF EXPENSE

There are 2 methods of getting Junior through Princeton currently making the rounds. Both seem quite workable. But (as with all such matters) do check this out with your accountant.

Method 1: The Interest-Free Loan. If you should have some income-producing property, simply lend it to Junior—interest free. Then your bright-eyed lad will be able to collect the income from your gift and use it for tuition.

For example: If you should have a spare $100,000 that's in a money market fund, earning 17 percent, you lend the $100,000 to your youngster (because it's not legal to *give* him more than $3000 a year, tax free, according to the IRS) and let him make the $17,000 that's earned from the principal. Of course, he will have to pay taxes. But, since this is his only source of income, he'll be paying at a much lower rate. And he can use the $17,000 (or what's left after taxes) to pay for college.

Method 2: The Ten-Year Trust. Take that $100,000 and set up a trust for the time Junior will be in college. Transfer the trust to him for this time. He uses the income to pay for school. Then, when the trust runs out, it reverts back to you.

The nifty thing about the second method is that you can start early—and accumulate money for Junior's education. If he's going to college in 1990, you start your trust in 1984, and then have six years during which the trust gets richer, so your boy or girl will have more money for school when he or she goes.

Both of these could be invalid if President Reagan fulfills a promise he made in his re-election platform. He said that tuition should be tax deductible. If that happens, then all your problems will be solved. Just consult your local newspaper for the latest developments.

HOW TO SET UP A TRUST AND GIVE YOUR CHILD A TAX-FREE EDUCATION

College costs are increasing rapidly. If you have a large amount set aside for your children's education, the taxes you pay on interest may wipe out a good portion of it. But by setting up a trust fund, you can save quite a bit in taxes. Here's how it works:

A Short-Term Trust. Also known as a Clifford trust, the money in a short-term trust is turned over to a trustee, and your child becomes the beneficiary. Interest will be compounded into the trust until the child reaches majority age.

How It Saves You Tax Dollars. Your child becomes legally responsible to pay the interest tax, but he or she also gets a personal exemption, which should be more than the interest. You can still use him as a deduction, too, as long as you are providing half of his support.

You Get the Principal Back. When your child reaches legal age (eighteen or twenty-one, depending on the state) he or she gets all of the interest earned while the trust was in effect, and you get the original investment. Since you and your spouse can give $6000 tax free to each of your children and not pay gift tax, your financial situation has not been impaired.

3 Things to Know:

1. If you plan to set up a trust, get a lawyer.
2. Have a clause placed in the trust agreement that entitles you to borrow from the principal, as long as you can put up adequate collateral. This will protect you against any unexpected financial crises.
3. You can arrange the trust so the child receives the income annually or when he or she reaches legal age. The child's financial situation dictates which is more beneficial. If he receives it annually, he pays taxes at his personal tax rate. If the money is held back, the trust pays it at individual rates. Check with your accountant.

COLLEGE SCHOLARSHIPS

Each year, hundreds of thousands of dollars in scholarship money is passed up because peopie just aren't aware that they exist. This problem has spawned a new industry designed to help the prospective college student—scholarship search organizations. These organizations have computer listings of every scholarship available. And for a fee they will match students to particular grants—depending on need, field of study, or extracurricular activities.

Here are 3 examples of offbeat scholarships that go begging every year, largely because they are unknown:

1. Yale has $1000 grants for students named Leavanworth or DeForest.

2. Juniata College has a number of grants for left-handed students.

3. One Arizona school has a scholarship waiting for a student who has roped calves.

You don't have to be a hulking football player or a budding nuclear physicist to get a scholarship. You just have to look a little harder to see what's available.

Two of the best-known services for information about scholarships are: Scholarship Search, 800 Huyler, Teterboro, NJ 07608, (201)228-2500; and Octameron Associates, P.O. Box 3437, Alexandra, VA 22302. Ask for their booklet, *The A's and B's of Merit Scholarship* and *Don't Miss Out.*

The moral here is *investigate.* Don't let a potential scholarship get away.

ALTERNATIVE WAYS TO DEFRAY THE COST OF HIGHER EDUCATION

Many young people have had to work their way through college in the past. Today, the skyrocketing cost of higher education has forced students to come up with even better methods of reducing the burden on their families. Let's look at 5 ways in which students are earning money while earning a degree:

1. *Cooperative Education.* An increasing number of institutions are offering this type of education for financially strapped students. It allows them to alternate their classroom work with jobs in industry, and necessitates an extra year of study. Students, however, can earn almost half of their college costs in this manner.

2. *Three-Year Degree Programs.* By passing advanced placement tests, some students can waive enough credits to graduate in three years instead of four, saving 25 percent of college expenses.

3. *Grants.* Most institutions offer individual financial aid plans for families with more than one child in college at the same time. Many parents, however, fail to take advantage of such opportunities, assuming they earn too much money to qualify. The income requirements, as a matter of fact, are quite high—even if you earn as much as $40,000 a year or more, you can be eligible for financial aid.

4. *Student Loans.* National Direct Student Loans are still available from the government at a very low interest rate. There have been some changes in the system because of abuses by some students (filing for bankruptcy after graduation, for example) but they are still universally available. These loans do not have to be repaid until after you graduate. In addition, a number of institutions offer loans at rates lower than the federal government.

5. *Shared Costs.* There is no way to cut the fixed costs of items such as tuition, but money can be saved in housing and book buying. Many students share apartments off campus, where three or four people can live instead of two in a dorm. Many colleges also buy and sell used textbooks, which can save a student an additional $100 or so per term.

College costs will continue to rise for a number of reasons. At publicly supported institutions, the budget is at the mercy of state legislatures looking to cut spending. At private schools, endowments can't keep up with inflation. Add the rising costs of energy, teacher and staff salaries, and you can see why more and more people are being priced out of higher education.

5. MEDICAL EXPENSES

SAVE ON MEDICAL EXPENSES

Medical expenses are the highest-priced services required today. A checkup, EKG, X rays, lab work, and a physical can cost between $300 and $400. With a family involved, medical care becomes a major expense.

The advice of many doctors nowadays is to skip that annual checkup. There is feeling in the medical profession that the results from these checkups are inconclusive. Dr. Michael McGinnis, of the U.S. Public Health Service in Washington, says, "Two things seem clear: periodic health visits can be useful, and annual physicals are not an effective way to structure those visits."

The American Heart Association and the American Cancer Society have admitted that annual checkups have not been able to prevent the rise in deaths from cancer or heart problems. According to the AHA, about half of all heart attacks occur in persons who have exhibited no prior symptoms of heart trouble.

On the other hand, many doctors are in favor of annual visits.

Often patients will not be aware of when they aren't feeling well. Dr. Isadore Rosenfeld, author of *The Complete Medical Exam,* stresses that "the interview between patient and doctor is more important than test results."

Here are 5 tips to keep in mind before seeing a doctor:

1. *Don't Change Doctors.* Your best bet is to choose one physician and stick with him or her, provided he or she gives you the type of treatment you need and want. Reputation is probably the best method. Find out if the doctor keeps regular office hours, is available in an emergency, and if he or she is affiliated with a local hospital. This will give you a good indication of the kind of doctor he or she is.

2. *Preventive Medicine Is Essential.* If you wait until you are seriously ill to see your doctor, you'll be setting yourself up for some hefty bills. An annual physical will allow your doctor to better understand your health needs. The early detection of any problem will give you a better chance of controlling or curing it. Emergencies are always more expensive than regular, preventive care.

3. *Don't Be Afraid to Discuss Fees.* Some doctors, if you ask them prior to examination, offer sliding scale fees or extended payments. This is especially true for specialists or surgeons, whose services are generally more expensive than the family physician's.

4. *Don't Beat Down Your Doctor's Office Door.* You can probably save yourself time, money, and aggravation if you use the telephone. What you think is an impending heart attack may very well turn out to be severe indigestion. Your doctor knows your medical history, and that information, plus the symptoms you describe over the phone, can help him or her assess the situation. If it's serious enough, he'll tell you to come in or to go to the hospital.

5. *Get Second Opinions.* It never hurts to get a second, or even

third opinion. One of the phenomena resulting from higher medical costs has been allegations of unnecessary surgery. If a specialist says you need an operation, don't take his or her word for it. Go to another doctor. You'll have to pay another examination fee, but it's a lot cheaper than going through an operation you don't need.

6.
CREDIT CARDS AND LOANS

SOME FACTS YOU SHOULD KNOW ABOUT CREDIT CARDS

Owning credit cards may be more expensive than you think. In addition to an annual fee that many banks charge, there is a finance charge on your outstanding balance. This charge may appear small when looking at the percentage points, but over a year, this can add up. The added sum of the annual fee and the finance charge may be more than you care to spend.

Now some banks are also charging a small fee for each card purchase made, which may make you think twice each time you want to use your card. Some banks don't permit you to pay your bill in full within twenty-five to thirty days without a finance charge.

Other banks, in order to attract more customers, offer special deals with their credit cards. For instance, one bank lets their cardholders earn credits each time their card is used. These credits go toward the purchase of discount merchandise from a catalogue.

It is best to look at each card individually, weighing the advantages and convenience of owning a particular card against the various service charges, annual fees, and finance charges. Unfortunately, charges change rapidly, so today's good deal may not be quite as good tomorrow. Keep your eye open for future opportunities to save money, and be sure you understand completely the regulations pertaining to your present card or cards.

HOW TO ESTABLISH CREDIT

If you have never had credit before, there are 6 steps you should take in case you ever have to take out a bank loan.

1. Maintain a checking account and be sure you don't bounce checks.

2. Open a savings account and make small deposits at regular intervals.

3. Apply for charge accounts at leading department stores. Use them and pay the bills on time. (If you are just beginning to establish credit, you may be given a limit on what you can charge.)

4. Apply for gasoline credit cards. Sometimes these are easier to obtain than store accounts.

5. After you have had your checking account for a while, attempt to get overdraft checking (whereby banks will cover overdrawn checks up to a certain amount). This feature is offered by most major banks. Although you may never have to use it, the fact that you can looks good on other credit applications.

6. If you are rejected for a charge account, the law says you have a right to know why. The details for obtaining such credit information are usually included in the rejection letter. It's important to find out why you are being rejected, because the information could be false.

BATTLING CREDIT CARD BILLING ERRORS

Almost everyone agrees about how terrific credit cards are—that is, except when you have to deal with a billing error. Billing mistakes can be a nightmare—especially if you're charged for a visit to a massage parlor or a $600 dress your wife swears she didn't buy. There is, however, recourse you can take to rectify credit card mistakes. The step-by-step process is as follows, as outlined by the Fair Credit Billing Act of 1974:

1. Write a letter of complaint to the credit card company. An address for billing errors is on your statement. The letter must be written within sixty days after you receive the bill and should include your address and account number. Also, be very specific about the charges that do not belong to you.
2. Make copies of every document that you send to the credit card company and make sure all of the material is dated.
3. You must be notified within thirty days that your complaint has been received.
4. Action on the complaint must be taken within ninety days.
5. While the billing error is being investigated, you do not have to pay the disputed portion of the bill.
6. If it turns out that the bill was in fact a mistake, you are entitled to a refund for any finance charges paid on it.
7. If the credit card company produces evidence that you do owe money, you will probably have to pay retroactive finance charges.
8. If the credit company does not follow the proper measures (as stated by law) you can elect not to pay $50 or the disputed portion of the bill—whichever is less. Then get yourself a lawyer. You probably have grounds for a suit against the company.

A closing note: In 1977, the Federal Reserve did a study and found out that less than 17 percent of all credit card holders knew there was a law regarding billing errors. What you don't know can in fact hurt you.

WHAT YOU SHOULD KNOW ABOUT THE TRUTH IN LENDING ACT

According to the law, borrowers have the right to certain information on any contract they sign. If you ever borrow money, open a charge account, or agree to pay for something in installments, the following information should be on the agreement. If it isn't, don't sign anything. In *Everyone's Money Book* (New York: Delacorte, 1978), Jane Bryant Quinn lists 7 things to remember:

1. Finance charge. This is not just the amount of the loan. It includes interest charges, service fees, handling charges, and other payments related to the handling of your account. Credit life insurance, if required, should also be listed. This part of the law, by the way, does not apply to mortgages.
2. Annual percentage rates. The annual percentage rate is the total finance charge in percentages, not dollars. This is to prevent unscrupulous lenders from using come-ons like "7 percent add-on." This portion of the law does include mortgages.
3. Repossession. The contract must state what, if any, property can be seized or repossessed by the lender if you don't pay up.
4. Late payment charges. The lender must list, in detail, any extra charges you will incur for not paying the bill on time.
5. Your right to cancel. The contract must state under exactly what circumstances you can change your mind and cancel the contract.
6. Balloon payments. These are extra payments tacked on after you've paid "the low monthly rate." These payments can catch

you off guard, so make sure they are detailed in the contract.

7. If the contract you sign is in violation of the Truth in Lending Act, you can sue for twice the amount of the finance charge as long as the amount does not exceed $1000.

These laws were created to protect you against unscrupulous lenders. Yet, most people don't even know they exist. If you are planning on getting credit of any kind, make sure the contract spells out your obligation—if not it spells trouble.

7. SMART SHOPPING

8 RULES FOR SHOPPING BY MAIL

Ordering products by mail can be an easy way to shop. It can also be aggravating if you don't do it properly. Here are 8 rules to follow:

1. Order well in advance of the date you want the product delivered, especially during the holidays.

2. Make sure to include your name, address, and other required information. Double and triple check the order form to be sure you are sending for the right product.

3. Order only from firms that you are familiar with or from companies that belong to an industry trade association. If you aren't sure, the Better Business Bureau can help.

4. Pictures can be misleading. Read the product description thoroughly to make sure you're getting what you want.

5. Understand the return and guarantee policies before ordering. If it explicitly says that all sales are final and you aren't satisfied with the product, you're stuck.

6. Do not pay by cash. It can easily get stolen in the mail. A canceled check is your best protection if merchandise isn't received.

7. When the package arrives, make sure the product is exactly what you ordered and that it is in perfect working order.

8. If you have a complaint and get no satisfaction within a few weeks, contact the Postal Inspection Service. They can start an investigation into mail fraud. Let any mail-order trade groups know about the bad apple in their tree. It may speed results.

---

10 THINGS YOU SHOULD KNOW ABOUT WARRANTIES

In this age of consumer protection, many manufacturers offer warranties for their products. It requires them to fix a product, to your satisfaction, for the period the warranty is in force. There are 10 things to look out for, though:

1. *Full Warranties*. Any product that carries a full warranty must be serviced, at no charge to you, for the life of the warranty. If the product is not fixed properly after a reasonable number of tries, the manufacturer is legally obligated to replace it.

2. *Limited Warranties*. Anything that isn't a full warranty is limited, and it must state exactly that on the warranty card. It may be limited regarding the particular parts that can be serviced or the time period involved.

3. *Implied Warranty*. No manufacturer is obligated to offer a warranty for its product. There is, however, an implied guarantee that the product will do the job it was bought for.

4. *Shipping Costs*. If you must pay for shipping and handling when returning a product for service, the warranty must say so. Normally, large items such as stereo speakers can be shipped at the manufacturer's expense.

5. *Operating Procedure*. There must be information providing the name and address of the company or authorized service representative and the procedure for having repair work done.

6. *Warranty on Record*. The retailer is obligated to carry a

copy of the warranty so you can see it before buying. He may assure you it's in the box, but you have a right to see it anyway.

7. *Arbitration Boards.* Arbitration boards are now available to handle complaints that the manufacturer won't resolve. Any information regarding such procedures must be listed on the warranty card.

8. *Warranties May Not Cover All Parts.* This is usually applicable to certain glass or plastic parts. They may not cost much to fix, but the labor involved may make such repairs prohibitive.

9. *Labor May Not Be Included.* The most expensive part of any repair work may not be covered by the manufacturer. If labor is not included, it must specifically state that on the warranty card.

10. *Mail Your Card In.* Although in most cases you don't need to do this to get service, it's still a good idea. If you make it a practice of not mailing these cards in, make sure the warranty doesn't require it.

Consumer protection laws have been strengthened in recent years, so there is no reason for you to get ripped off. If, however, you abuse a product and then attempt to get it repaired, look for trouble. Most manufacturers will honor their warranty. They want your repeat business.

HOW AND WHERE TO COMPLAIN ABOUT A PRODUCT

You have a right to complain if a product you purchased doesn't work properly. There are 10 ways to go about it, however, which can make resolution of the problem easier:

1. *Contact the Merchant.* Be courteous but firm. Explain the problem, give the date the item was purchased, and supply all the necessary details. Make a note of the date you called and

always get the name of the person you spoke to. Follow up the phone call with a letter and keep a copy of it. If you are dealing with a department store or chain store, a customer relations department might be a good place to start.

2. *Contact the President of the Company*. If contacting someone at the store level does not resolve your problem, write a letter to the president. Enclose your original letter, with an additional letter citing the fact that your request was ignored. Don't be sarcastic. The president probably doesn't know anything about your situation, so why prejudice him or her against you from the beginning?

3. *Go to an Outside Agency*. If your request is ignored by the president, contact an organization like the Better Business Bureau or the Chamber of Commerce. Include all of your correspondence with the retailer, and be specific about the problem. Do the same with any consumer protection agency in your area, particularly those at the most local of levels. Each of these groups could provide assistance by writing the company in your behalf.

4. *Write the Manufacturer*. Even if the retailer ignores your pleas, you may find a sympathetic ear from the manufacturer. You did, of course, purchase his or her product, and the store's behavior is a direct reflection on him. He may be able to push the retailer into action, especially if your complaint isn't the first.

5. *Contact State and Federal Agencies*. Your state consumer protection agency or a federal agency like the Federal Trade Commission may take a long time to respond to your problem, but they could be valuable assets if a class-action suit is filed, for example. If you don't tell them about shady practices, they'll never know, and that merchant will continue to operate as usual.

6. *Contact the Post Office*. The Post Office employs inspectors

for mail fraud cases, which include consumer complaints about products that were never received or damaged goods.

7. *Go to the Media.* A local newspaper, radio station, or television show may have a reporter who acts as a consumer watchdog. Because of the media's influence with the public, a reporter with a pen or microphone might get faster results than a government agency with its paperwork and regulations.

8. *Contact Trade Associations*. Some industries, through their trade associations, may have complaint bureaus for you to air your problems. A list of all of these groups, along with addresses and phone numbers, is available in a book called *The Encyclopedia of Associations*. You can find it at the library.

9. *Contact Professional Associations*. Complaints against professionals are much harder to resolve, but you can make your voice heard by contacting a group like the local bar association or a county medical society.

10. *Write Complaint Letters to the Manufacturer.* Include the following in any letter of complaint: your name, address, and phone number; the name, address, and phone number of the merchant; date of the purchase and the exact nature of the problem, dates on which complaints were made, and any such correspondence. If possible, include documents such as invoices or warranty cards. Also specify what you want done, be it a repair, a replacement, or a refund.

RENTING MAY SAVE YOU MONEY

With the high cost of everything today, many people are finding it practical to rent rather than buy items they use only occasionally or need for a limited time. And often it is easy to do. There are six to eight thousand rental stores in the United States and Canada. Check "Rental Service" in the Yellow Pages and the "Rental" section under the product you are interested in.

When renting equipment, a deposit is usually required, depending on the length of rental time and the value of the merchandise. It is a good idea to have the rental rate, overtime charges, and guarantees in writing.

8. DIVORCE

Although almost no one deliberately plans for a divorce, in today's society too often divorce turns out to be a fact of life. The following pages provide tips to keep in mind should you be so unfortunate as to find yourself in the midst of divorce proceedings.

---

6 WAYS TO REDUCE THE COST OF A DIVORCE

A divorce can be an expensive proposition. But should it be necessary, here are 6 things you and your spouse can do to make the procedure smoother and less costly:

1. *Negotiate When Possible.* The more you fight about property, alimony, and the children, the higher your legal fees will be. An uncontested action is obviously the cheapest way to get a divorce settlement.

2. *Be Realistic.* Don't raise your expectations about what you can get to a ridiculous level. Your lawyer should know how the courts in your area make awards in divorce proceedings. Avoid

lawyers who promise the moon: they're just looking to pump up their fees.

3. *Avoid Litigation.* If at all possible, reach a settlement out of court. Court battles can be expensive and time consuming. You may also be able to come to terms over matters that the court cannot legally decide on—private schools, orthodontal work, etc.

4. *Avoid a Legal Separation.* Not all states allow you to file for a divorce directly, but if it's possible, do it. Legal fees for a separation can be expensive.

5. *Consider a Do-It-Yourself Divorce.* Many states are adopting this method as a way of reducing the backlog in the courts. In states where it is legal, you won't even need a lawyer.

6. *Be Mature.* If you approach the divorce in a mature fashion, you'll probably be able to divide your property, decide on alimony, and agree on child support with a minimum amount of fighting. It will make the settlement easier and save you money in the long run.

HOW A DIVORCE AFFECTS YOUR TAX RETURN

If you thought the divorce was rough, wait till you attempt to do your tax return. After you've paid the lawyers, court costs, alimony, and child support, the IRS is waiting with open hands. Negotiations between former husbands and wives can ease the tax burden, but many couples are tired of battling when they've left the courtroom. Here's how IRS feels about your divorce:

1. *The House.* For most couples, this is the most expensive possession. If the husband turns over his share of the home to his spouse, the IRS sees it as a "sale" of sorts, and expects a capital gains tax on his share of the profit. Example: you pur-

chased your house for $50,000, and it's worth $80,000 at the time of the divorce. The capital gain was $30,000, the husband's "profit" half that. No money exchanged hands, but capital gains of $15,000 are taxed.

You can defer payment of these taxes by purchasing a new home, or, if you are over fifty-five, use the once-in-a-lifetime tax exemption of up to $100,000. You can also change your residency status to "tenancy in common" with an agreement that your wife will get the profit when the house is sold. In exchange, you will get some of that money to pay any capital gains tax at the point of sale.

2. *Alimony.* The government is more lenient when it comes to alimony. It is tax deductible (child support is not) and most tax experts in this area recommend the husband pay as much deductible support as he can. The wife, on the other hand, should make sure the alimony she receives doesn't push her into a higher tax bracket. One thing to keep in mind: alimony is not deductible if the spouse receiving it doesn't pay taxes.

3. *Unallocated Support Payments.* This is a fairly new method of easing the tax burden at the time of divorce. The "payments" are a lump sum for both alimony and child support, but since it is considered "unallocated" (unspecific as to how it's divided) the IRS allows for a deduction on the entire amount.

Remember, negotiation is the best way to avoid both spouses' getting socked by the government. Both can usually get what they want, and more, since the IRS will be taking less.

9. TRAVEL

You look forward to those vacation weeks every year, yet plane fares and travel costs make it difficult for many people to afford, so they stay home instead of taking that European trip they've always dreamed about. In this segment you'll find suggestions for cutting those vacation costs, shopping around for a deal on a rental car, cutting your hotel expenses, and new types of low-cost vacations. There's no reason for you to give up that dream vacation—you just have to shop around a bit more.

A NIFTY WAY TO CUT VACATION EXPENSES

Are you looking for a clever and inexpensive way to travel all over the world? Try house-swapping. Here's how it works: You arrange to stay in someone else's house while they stay in yours. House-swapping is a marvelous way to kill two birds with one stone: you have an opportunity to get out of the house and see new places, and your house is watched over for you while you're gone. There are, however, 4 ground rules that may help you to make this venture more enjoyable and profitable:

1. First, decide whether you want to take in the Broadway shows of Manhattan or sail on the Cape. Pick your vacation spot and start looking for swappers.

2. There are many ways to find out about people interested in house-swapping. You can advertise in the *New York Review of Books* or local newspapers and magazines of the area you are interested in staying in. However, the best sources of information are probably the house-swapping services such as the Vacation Exchange Club, 12006 111th Ave., Youngtown, Arizona, the Home Interchange Ltd. (Britain), and the Shalom Israhouse (Israel).

3. Check your insurance coverage. If you merely swap your house with another person, he or she is considered your guest, and it is very likely that your insurance covers you. If you charge rent, however, it is likely that you need special coverage to protect your possessions and property. Liability insurance should also be considered.

4. Once you have found people who are interested, correspond with them asking for details about their home and providing information about yours. Make certain that you both are fully aware of the comforts and drawbacks of the exchange. Photographs and floor plans provide good information about the amount of space available, for example.

House-swapping is one of the most exciting ways to have an enjoyable and comfortable vacation in the United States and throughout the world.

HOW TO CUT YOUR HOTEL BILLS

Aside from your air fare, hotel expenses are probably the largest you'll have on your trip. Despite misconceptions, there are ways you can reduce your hotel bills without suffering in fleabags. Here are 7 hints:

1. *Ask for a Room by Category.* Most hotels list their prices by category: economy, standard, and luxury. If you want the lowest rate, ask for it. Amenities such as air conditioning, television, and phone service are generally provided, regardless of the room charge. There is also a chance, if the hotel isn't booked, that you'll get a better room at no extra charge.

2. *Avoid Room Service.* You can save money by eating in the hotel restaurant instead of ordering room service. The food is generally the same, but the prices aren't. In addition, there is usually an extra room-service charge.

3. *Know When Checkout Time Is.* Checkout time can be inconvenient, so if you want to stay a few extra hours, ask the manager. If the hotel isn't booked, your room won't be needed at once, and you can probably stay without an additional charge.

4. *Inquire About Family Plans.* If you are traveling with children, ask about any type of family plan. Sometimes a folding cot will be provided at a nominal cost, much less than the charge for an extra room.

5. *Phone Ahead to Confirm or Make Reservations.* Most large hotels or chains have toll-free numbers which you can use to make or confirm reservations for your next stop. It may not seem like a large amount of money to phone or wire ahead on the road, but it does add up.

6. *Cut Ground Transportation Expenses.* Your hotel may offer shuttle bus service, free or for a nominal fee, to the airport at regular intervals. If not, there may be an airport bus which stops

at your hotel. Either way is probably cheaper than a taxi. Advance planning in this regard can be very valuable.

7. *Check Out the Older Hotels.* Many people have a preconceived notion that older hotels are more expensive because of their reputation. This isn't always the case, and you may be surprised to find that older hotels may be cheaper than a chain.

There are other tips you can use to cut your travel expenditures, such as vacationing during the off-season or during the week. You'll have more money to spend on the important parts of your trip: sightseeing, gifts, or meals in fine restaurants.

HOW TO SAVE MONEY TRAVELING IN EUROPE

Trains are generally considered the best method of traveling through Europe if you want to see a good deal of the continent. But there can be problems. These 7 tips can help you avoid needless expense and aggravation:

1. *Consider a Eurailpass.* A Eurailpass is a card sold by United States travel agents which allows you an unlimited number of train rides for a set period of time. It's a flat rate, and it can be very economical considering the cost of a single trip tickets. If you're under twenty-six you can buy a second-class youth pass good for one month for $290 (or two months for $370). If you're over twenty-six you can buy a first-class pass good for fifteen days for $260 (or one month for $410). A Eurailpass, however, does not guarantee you a seat. You must make a reservation at the station or through a travel agent, usually no more than twenty-four hours before the train departs. Such a reservation costs a nominal fee of $2.

2. *Plan Ahead for Overnight Accommodations.* A berth can, and should be, reserved in advance. It won't afford much privacy, but the cost ($10 to $15) is cheaper than most European hotel rooms. A private compartment, designed for one or two persons, is $75.

3. *Read the Signs.* Since train travel is the most common type of transportation throughout Europe, most stations provide readily visible and detailed posters listing all arrivals and departures. Such information is generally available on a twenty-four-hour basis. Remember, however, that the information is based on the European system of indicating time: 14:40, for example, is 2:40 P.M. When you board, check the sign in your car to make sure it goes all the way to your destination. Some interconnected systems require through trains to drop off cars en route. If you do not see such a sign, ask the first conductor or ticket-taker you see.

4. *Be Careful About Getting Off.* Even if your timetable indicates a sizable wait at a particular station, don't leave the train for too long. In dropping off or picking up cars, the train may switch tracks several times, making it potentially difficult for you to locate your train.

5. *Plan Ahead Where Food and Drink Are Concerned.* Most European trains do not have drinking water aboard, dining cars are added infrequently, and vendors are not always available. Stock up on beverages and food at the station before departing. If your train is passing through several countries, make sure you have local currency for each stop. If a vendor shows up, chances are only local currency will be accepted.

6. *Travel Light.* Do not pack too heavily. European train stations, unlike major airports, provide little or no assistance with luggage. You may be able to find a porter in major stations, but it won't help if you need to catch a train in a hurry. A set of wheels or casters which you can attach to your luggage will be

extremely helpful. Carrying your luggage from platform to train, up stairways, etc., can be back-breaking.

7. *Plan Your Trip in Advance.* July and August are the worst months for European travel, because that's when most of the natives take their vacations. *Europe by Eurail,* updated annually by the publisher (George W. Ferguson, Box 20334, Columbus, Ohio 43220), is a useful guide. Another must is the *Thomas Cook International Timetable,* available from the Forsyth Travel Library, Box 2975, Shawnee Mission, Kansas 66201.

VACATION AT AN OVERSEAS UNIVERSITY: AN EXCITING WAY TO TRAVEL

If you're tired of routine sightseeing tours and hotels, there's a new way to vacation in Europe. By studying at a foreign university like Cambridge, even for just one week, you can learn, see the country, and cut your travel expenses at the same time. And if the class you take is related to your job, air fare and travel costs can be tax deductible.

Who Offers These Study Vacations? Many programs are offered by American colleges and universities; others are handled by the European institution. You need not, however, be a student to take advantage of such programs.

Where Are They Held? Traditional classroom studies are held in colleges and universities such as Oxford, Cambridge, and Edinburgh; archeological tours are available in such distant countries as Morocco, Tunisia, Egypt, and Israel; language study programs are offered around the world; sailing tours of Greece and the Caribbean and other seacoasts are also available.

What Is the Cost? Expenses vary, but most courses include tuition, room, and board. Transportation is extra. A three-week session at Oxford is less than $1500 and includes tuition, room, and meals. Other programs are less than $900 for two weeks.

How Do I Apply? A helpful book on study programs is *Vacation Study Abroad,* available through the Institute of International Education, 809 UN Plaza, New York, New York 10017 (212-883-8200). Apply early. Space fills up fast.

10.
TAXES

You get a raise and suddenly you find the government with its hand out, looking for more tax dollars. You don't want to cheat the IRS, but you feel you're entitled to your hard-earned dollars.

There are ways you can cut taxes, and in this chapter we will explore these possibilities, offering valuable hints about tax shelters, trust funds, and other types of tax-free income. Can you make a million dollars and not pay taxes? Is there anything you can do to reduce your estate taxes? How do you pick an accountant or tax preparer? Many of us complain about higher taxes, yet most of us don't take full advantage of the tax laws. Read on to find out how.

HOW TO MAKE A MILLION AND NOT PAY TAXES

Is It Legal? One man who earns more than a million dollars a year and pays no taxes says everything he does is above board. Through constant surveillance, he is able to measure every penny of his income against everything he can write off. No schemes, no fraud. Just some old-fashioned ingenuity.

What's the Secret? The best way to save on taxes is by continually planning. You should, of course, know exactly what you have in taxable income and keep an up-to-date list. Once a month is probably sufficient for most people. If you see, for example, that you have a sizable net income after the first quarter (one which would put you in the 50 percent tax bracket), it's time to look for investments you can use as a write-off. Energy development, for example. If you wait too long, a good investment may pass you by or the IRS won't allow you the write-off for the entire year. When looking for such investments, say the experts, try to find the profitable ones. There's no sense losing money you're going to write off.

How Large Should the Deduction Be? Most people who play this game will tell you not to make a deductible investment unless the deductible is at least two times greater than the initial cash outlay. That is, a write-off on an investment of $5000 should provide a deduction of at least $10,000.

Can You Do It Yourself? You probably could, but you won't reap all of the potential benefits that a knowledgeable financial counselor can. Your investments must be well researched and properly timed.

It May Be Legal, But Is It Ethical? The people who do this think so. They feel that investment credits and deductions are there for the public to take advantage of, despite some of the risk involved. In essence, the government is handing off the ball like a good quarterback would. And as long as there's a hole, why not run for daylight?

A PERSONAL STRATEGY FOR TAX SAVINGS—10 THINGS YOU SHOULD BE DOING

Here are 10 strategies you can use that will strip away some excess tax baggage and help you to take full advantage of the laws:

1. Wait until the end of the year to make charitable contributions. By waiting, you can generally tell whether your income is high or low enough to justify them.

2. Time your cash payments. There are some predictable annual expenses that are deductible. If you can arrange to have these bills come due in December, you can decide whether to pay immediately and take the deduction for the current year or wait until January to pay them. The IRS considers a bill paid when the check is mailed.

3. By intentionally overpaying state and local income tax estimated installments, you can shift your tax burden from one year to the next. The federal government will allow a deduction for overpayment to be taken in the year it was paid. The refund, however, won't count as income until you get it.

4. Prepayment of state income tax. The IRS will allow a deduction in the current year if you pay your state income tax before the year ends. You can use this strategy to reduce your personal income because the deduction for the higher state tax will go in the same year you report a high gross income to the feds.

5. If possible, alternate your medical expenses from year to year. In this way, every other year you can double what might otherwise be a low annual medical deduction. It works this way: You are allowed to deduct any medical expenses that exceed 3 percent of your gross income. To push medical expenses into the next year, schedule dental, eye, and physical examinations for December. If you pay the bills in January, you can take the deduction in the next tax year.

6. Offset any capital gains or losses by selling other assets. For example, long-term gains can be offset for tax purposes by short-term losses. Check the tax books available or consult your investment adviser or accountant for details.

7. Alternate itemizing and taking standard deductions year by year. You will always come out ahead if you shift itemized deductions. Example: In each of two tax years you take $5000 in itemized deductions, a total of $10,000 over two years. If, however, you could shift $4000 for one year to the next, and take the maximum standard deduction of $2300 (for a single taxpayer) in the other, you get $11,300 in deductions.

8. Use the $10,000 gift tax exclusion. If you file a joint return, you can give $10,000 per person tax free. It not only reduces your taxes, it reduces your estate.

9. Schedule payment of deductible expenses at the end of the year. Things like investment counseling, safety deposit boxes, and business related expenses. At that point, you'll know whether you want to shift them into the next tax season.

10. If you can legally prepay real estate taxes, do it. It will give you the chance to get the deduction when you need it most.

TAX COMPUTATION

The most grueling and discouraging part of filing your tax return is figuring out how much you *owe* the federal government. One way to cut the tax bill is by income averaging, however, and we'll take a look at it.

Computing Your Tax. You can use the Tax Tables in the back of the Federal Income Tax instruction booklet if you meet any of the following standards (according to line 38 of form 1040, "Tax Table Income"):

1. Your taxable income is $50,000 a year or less.
2. You do not income average.
3. You do not file a short-period tax return because of a change in your annual accounting period.

If you do have over $50,000 in income, file a short-period tax return, or income average, you must use Tax Rate Schedules X, Y, or Z.

Income Averaging. If you get a large increase in income from one year to the next, you may be eligible for income averaging. Your one-year jump in income is handled as though it were received over a five-year period, each treated equally. Here's how it works: Your current taxable income must surpass by more than $3000 a figure that is 120 percent of your average income in the previous four years. For example, your current income is $25,000, and your average income over the past four years was $15,000. 120 percent of $15,000 is $18,000, which is $7,000 less than your present income. Therefore it would be to your advantage to income average.

Not Everyone Is Eligible. You may meet the mathematical requirements but not be able to income average. The IRS restricts this method to U.S. citizens or residents. Recent college graduates, as well as persons who recently entered the labor force, may also be ineligible.

A Final Word. Because of budget limitations, the IRS has not included tax tables in its publication "Your Federal Income Tax." For that reason, save your tax instruction booklet. It lists the tax computation tables which were deleted from Publication 17.

CHANGES IN THE TAX LAWS THAT AFFECT YOUR INVESTMENT STRATEGY

Every so often there are changes in the tax laws that relate to investors. If your holdings are small, you may tend to overlook these changes. Don't. They may prove valuable and can change your investment plans. A look at 4 of the more recent actions by Congress:

1. *Capital Gains.* A more lenient approach to capital gains means that many investors can profit by selling certain assets at the end of the year. Only 40 percent of the gain is now taxable, and the top tax rate applied to this taxable part had dropped to less than 30 percent. There is also a once-in-a-lifetime exclusion from gains tax for people over fifty-five who sell their homes. (Limit of the exclusion: $125,000)

The 15 percent minimum tax on the untaxed portion of capital gains has been eliminated, provided you have owned the assets for more than one year.

2. *Tax Shelter Investments.* This applies to almost all shelters except real estate and limits deductions to only your initial cash investment. The law now applies to shelter corporations that have a majority ownership of five or more individuals, making some limited partnerships less attractive than before.

Oil and gas shelters may benefit from a rule change regarding the taxation of labor and drilling charges. These charges were previously added to the tax "preference" list on earned income, but another amendment allows royalties from gas and oil finds to be deducted.

3. *Small Business.* Another recent change may help many unincorporated businesses. Owners of such establishments used to be able to categorize up to 30 percent of their income as personal service income, subject to the lesser 50 percent maximum tax. Now, however, a "reasonable amount" may be treated as per-

sonal service income, which can be 50 to 75 percent of the total net income.

Also, owners of small companies can now treat any losses as regular tax losses and use them to offset other high-taxed income up to $50,000.

4. *Home Ownership.* In addition to the one-time exclusion allowed in selling your home, capital gains taxes on the sale of a home can be forgiven provided you move into a new home within two years. Be careful, though: the law applies only to a principal residence, although the IRS has been known to allow the tax forgiveness for items like a yacht, provided it has cooking, sleeping, and sanitation facilities on board.

As you can see, ever-changing tax laws can affect the way you invest. Be aware of the changes before buying or selling anything. The knowledge may save you hundreds or thousands of dollars.

HOW TO SELL OFF MUNICIPAL BONDS TO SAVE TAXES

There are ways you can avoid suffering high taxes on gains you have made in the stock market. One is to establish tax-deductible losses than can offset taxable gains in the market. These 2 steps show you how the process works:

1. Sell your devalued municipal bonds at a loss to give you the tax deduction for the year.

2. Then use the proceeds to reinvest in other municipals that are tax exempt.

This sounds simple, but there are 6 other considerations:

1. The best yields are those with long-term gains.

2. Watch out for reinvestments that might be affected by another interest-rate cycle somewhere down the road.

3. Tax-exempt trusts are one of the more attractive alternative investments. Unit trusts, unlike the open-end managed bond-funds, have fixed portfolios. You can sell these units—at the market price—anytime before maturity.

4. Pay close attention to the tax rules. You have only up to December 31 to deduct for your devalued municipal bonds, for example. There are other rules that compel you to wait thirty days before you reinvest your proceeds.

5. It is safer if the bonds sold and bought have different issues and if the maturity dates are further apart.

6. Double check your gains and losses from the "swap" when you fill out your Form 1040.

See what opportunities are available and enjoy the money saved. But don't dawdle, the swap season is early this year!

USING TAX CREDITS TO CUT YOUR TAXES

Many Americans are using tax credits as a way to reduce their taxable income. They can range from charitable or political contributions to energy expenditures like home insulation to items purchased that you need for your job but the company won't pay for. Many of these credits are valuable to people in the higher tax brackets, but anyone can take advantage of them. Here are 4 of the most popular ones:

1. *Political Contributions.* The IRS will allow a credit on half of any contribution to a candidate for public office, up to a maximum credit of $50 ($100 on a joint tax return). The donation must have been monetary, however, so you can't deduct a random figure for volunteer work. In addition, the IRS will not honor a credit for contributions to organizations like NCPAC (National

Conservative Political Action Committee) that use the money to single out particular politicians for defeat.

2. *Energy Tax Credits.* Two types of credits were approved by Congress to encourage energy conservation. The first credit is for energy improvements in your home, and includes items like caulking, weather stripping, insulation, storm doors, and clock thermostats. The credit is good for 15 percent of the first $2000 spent, to a maximum of $300. The second credit is for costs of renewable energy improvements such as a solar heating system or wind powered electrical generator. The credit is good for 40 percent of the first $10,000 spent, up to $4000. The improvements must be made on your principal residence to be eligible for the tax credit. A credit will not be allowed for ones that are primarily aesthetic, such as wood-burning stoves, drapes, and carpeting.

3. *Tax Credit for the Elderly.* Senior citizens on Social Security or persons under sixty-five who get money from a public retirement plan may be eligible for a tax credit for the elderly. The credit is figured on a sliding scale based on income received from other sources. The laws are complex, so the IRS will calculate it, by mail, providing you include all of the necessary paperwork.

4. *Earned Income Credit.* This is designed for low-income workers with families. It is a credit in the form of a refund. You can get it even if you owe no taxes, but your income must be less than $10,000.

As you can see, there are a number of avenues, in the form of credits, that can help you reduce your tax bill. Most are not too complex, so you should make every effort to take advantage of them.

HOW TO PICK THE RIGHT TAX SHELTER

Because of the government's determination to reduce the amount of foreign oil coming into the United States, a number of tax shelters have become available to the investor. Here are 7 things to watch out for:

1. *Tax Credits Involve Some Highly Speculative Deals.* When Congress passed the windfall profits tax in 1980, a number of additional tax credits were introduced to spur development of alternate energy resources. On top of the usual 10 percent investment tax credit on productive capital, the government is offering an additional 10 to 15 percent credit on anything from solar and wind power to geothermal development. In other words, the government is effectively paying you back 20 to 25 percent of your investment in the year it was made. If you are unable to use these credits in the first year, you are allowed to go back three years to reduce taxes or to shelter yourself for the next seven.

2. *The Initial Investment May Be Large.* Since many of these deals involve relatively untested technology and large government subsidy, some developers have no interest in going through the complex disclosure and registration process which the Securities and Exchange Commission requires for a public offering. Private placement is often chosen, but that limits the number of investors to thirty-five. This increases the minimum investment to you—sometimes to as large as $50,000. There are also strict net worth and income requirements: normally larger than $100,000, not including the value of your home.

3. *Not All of These Investments Need Be Risky.* Due to the deregulation of oil (and, presumably, natural gas) there are a number of options open to you in conventional oil and gas drilling. Billions of dollars in development capital are raised through

publicly registered, limited-partnership plans each year. And that figure is certain to rise in the years ahead. The small risk, however, is that oil is becoming increasingly harder to find, and your dollars may go to exploration in lands that were considered to have little potential before the price hikes.

4. *There Is a Way to Reduce Risk, But the Return Will Be Lower.* Some oil companies, in an effort to reduce the risk to investors, now offer "royalty funds." In such a deal, you, as a limited partner, put up money only to purchase the drilling lease. You do not pay for the cost of drilling on that land or the costs of storing if the well comes in. Because the risk is limited, however, the return is too.

5. *Handling the Debt Is Key.* Debt leverage is essential to any successful tax shelter. You can structure the deal, for example, by investing $20,000, $15,000 of which you borrow from the developer. You get drilling-cost deductions and investment tax credits on the entire investment, however, not just the amount you put up front. These credits can be used to repay your cash investment, and income from the property will pay off the remainder of the debt.

6. *Letter-of-Credit Deals.* One sticking point with the Internal Revenue Service is its determination to refuse you the tax credit unless you are "at risk," or liable for the debt. One way to get around this is a letter-of-credit deal. Instead of borrowing from the developer, your bank agrees to vouch for your ability to pay if the funds are called. For a fee of 1 or 2 percent of the face value, most banks issue such letters rather freely. The developer then uses your letter to arrange his or her own financing. One consultant warns, however, that the chances of your funds being called are better than 50/50 because many drilling plans don't pay enough to finance the debt.

7. *Remember Who Made the Laws.* When considering a tax shelter, always keep in mind that the Congress which made the

laws favorable can always rescind them. If that happens, you may be setting yourself up for big tax problems. Or worse, your debt leverage will decrease, an essential point in any tax shelter.

FORM A FAMILY PARTNERSHIP AND CUT YOUR TAX BILL

If you have your own business and are tired of writing huge checks to the IRS, here's an idea that might help. Create a family partnership and split your income with relatives in a lower tax bracket. Remember these 8 rules:

1. A family partnership may include only a spouse, children, and grandparents. Inclusion of other relatives makes it a general partnership.
2. A child of any age can be a partner. If, however, the child is a minor, his or her share must be held in trust or under a guardianship.
3. Capital must play a part in producing income for a family member to become a partner. If you are in a service industry, the relative must perform a valuable service at regular intervals.
4. When you donate to the partnership, you must deduct a reasonable amount for your own salary. The remainder of the profit can then be divided among the partnership.
5. Your gift is subject to the gift tax, but you can circumvent that by turning over a share which is equal to $10,000 a year. The first $10,000 of any gift is excluded from taxation.
6. The partners' shares of the profits can be left in the business for expansion. The relative must, however, take out enough money to pay his or her taxes on the profit. If you pay your child's income tax, the payment might be considered a gift.

7. You can still take your child as a deduction, regardless of the amount of income he or she receives from the business.

8. Including your spouse in the partnership will not reduce your personal income tax, but it will help you reduce your estate.

THE CHARITABLE FOUNDATION, OR, HOW ANY MULTIMILLIONAIRE CAN GIVE HIMSELF OR HERSELF A $1,000,000 TAX DEDUCTION

If you have a large estate, you stand to make a lot of money by going into a charitable partnership with other family members. Specifically, by giving them portions of significant assets—real estate, stocks, oil and gas interests, etc.—you partially freeze the value of these assets. This means future growth in said assets passes to family members without the liability of gift and estate taxes. When you develop a charitable partnership, the assets in question are usually divided 3 ways:

1. One portion is kept by the donor—and frozen so it earns no interest (and, logically, pays no taxes).

2. A second portion is allotted to family members and is allowed to appreciate. This is the only portion that earns interest.

3. The third and final portion is donated to a charity—and is frozen in the same way the donor's portion is. When giving this third portion, the donor purchases life insurance in the amount of the gift. The life insurance is then used to buy off the charity's portion of the asset when the partnership is dissolved some fifteen to twenty years later.

There is basically only one qualification you need to meet in order to set up this type of financial arrangement. That is the amount of money you should have available to put into it. It is suggested that you place well over $1 million into the program. If you have $5 million to invest, for example, your three-way breakdown would be as follows: $1 million is kept by you, the donor; $2 million is given to family members; and $2 million is donated to charity. Assuming you're in the 50 percent tax bracket, this would give you a tax deduction of $1 million on the $2 million donated to charity.

11 WAYS TO DEDUCT YOUR HOBBY

You own racehorses. Collect stamps or coins. Can you deduct any expenses in excess of income? That depends on whether or not your hobby is considered a profitable business by the IRS. Here are 11 things the government takes into account to determine if your hobby is a business:

1. Do you keep complete accounting records?
2. What is the expertise of yourself and your advisers in the activity?
3. How much time do you spend on the hobby?
4. Can you expect assets to appreciate in value?
5. What is your previous track record in similar activities?
6. What is your profit compared to your investment and losses?
7. Is this your primary source of income?
8. Have you lost money over a time period longer than what's necessary to turn a profit?
9. How much personal pleasure do you get?
10. Do you get substantial tax benefits?
11. Do you get significant income from other sources?

If answers to these questions are indicative that your hobby is primarily a profit-making venture, you'll be okay.

POSTPONE PAYING TAXES ON THE SALE OF YOUR HOME

For millions of Americans, owning a home is the biggest protection they have against inflation. One reason is the encouragement offered by the tax laws.

Real estate taxes and mortgage interest are tax deductible every year, but there is also a way to postpone, indefinitely, the capital gains tax when you sell your home. Here's how:

The Requirements for Such a Break. There are, generally, 3 rules that the IRS applies to such postponement:

1. The house you sell, and the one you buy, must be considered your principal residence.

2. You must purchase and move into the new house within two years of the sale (before or after) of the old home. If you are building a new home, construction must begin with 18 months of the sale, occupation within two years.

3. The new home must cost at least as much as the amount you got from the sale. If it costs less than the old home, part or all of your capital gain is taxed. The tax rates in this area, however, are favorable.

Other Exclusions. Anyone fifty-five or over can take advantage of a "once-in-a-lifetime" exclusion that allows for the exclusion of up to $125,000 on the sale of a house. Apartments that are turned into condominiums may also be eligible for this exclusion.

Other Types of Residences Are Eligible for the Deferment. A single-family home is not the only type of residence on which you can take the postponement. The purchase of a mobile home, trailer, cooperative apartment, condominium, or sailboat is acceptable as long as that becomes your principal residence. In 1979 the IRS ruled that a yacht could also qualify, as long as it has sleeping, cooking, and sanitation facilities on board.

What to Report to Internal Revenue:

1. If there is no capital gain from the sales of your home, the transaction must still be reported.

2. If there is a capital gain but you will not be buying another residence, use the appropriate IRS form to compute the gain and to report it. Your accountant should be able to help provide the needed forms, or you may write to the IRS.

3. If there is a gain but you are undecided about another purchase (or it isn't complete), complete form 2119, show the sale on form 2119, part 2, and write "none" in the "gains" column. You must also attach a statement which computes the gain and indicates you have not made a decision regarding another residence.

4. If and when you purchase another residence (during the specified time period), file form 2119 with the IRS. If there is no gain to be taxed, just list the dates of occupancy, purchase, and the cost. If there is a taxable gain or you don't purchase another home during the specified limit, an amended return must be filed for the year of the original sale. You will then pay tax for the gain you deferred.

Maintain Good Records. Record keeping is essential in determining how much of a gain you realize on the sale of a house. The actual gain you realize is the amount of the sale minus the tax cost. The tax cost is very important. It includes such things as legal fees, broker commissions, "points" paid by the seller, as well as any external or internal improvements you may have made prior to selling the house. Any additions, extended driveways, central air-conditioning, finished basements, etc., go into reducing your capital gain, and of course, the tax you pay.

8 TIPS FOR REDUCING ESTATE TAXES

If you have a reasonably large estate, you probably understand the tax implications to your beneficiaries. Here are 8 tips:

1. *How Much Can I Give?* According to the laws, you can make gifts of $10,000 per year per recipient tax free. These gifts would not be included in your taxable estate, although the recipients must pay income tax on them. You are exempt from a gift tax.

2. *Can I Give More?* The only way for you to increase your gift is on a joint basis. If your wife agrees, for example, you can give a total of $20,000 a year per recipient.

3. *What Is the Time Limit on Gifts?* You can make these gifts only once a year. If you skip a year, for instance, you cannot compensate by giving $20,000 the next. The exclusion is good for one year only.

4. *A Change in the Tax Laws.* Since 1976, the Federal Gift Tax, which can be as high as 70 percent, had been combined with the Federal Estate Tax to form one "credit." The credit, now $79,300, is reduced every time a gift is made. At the time of death, however, the remainder of the credit can be used against any Federal Estate Tax. Estates smaller than $275,000 are exempt from taxes.

5. *Be Careful About the Amount of Gifts You Give.* One problem that gift givers run into can be a serious one—depleting their estates in order to reduce the tax burden on their children. Just because the $10,000 annual exclusion exists, don't feel obligated to make use of it.

6. *Are There Any Special Tax Returns Which Must Be Filed?* Those with modest estates may be able to give more than $10,000 a year because of the "unified credit" and not be subject to a gift tax. You must, however, continue to file a Gift Tax Return, Form 709, or short form 709-A. The purpose of this form, which

is for persons who do not owe taxes on gifts, is to ensure that the spouse has consented to make a joint gift. You may have tax problems if one spouse dies without having filed these forms.

7. *What About Nonmonetary Gifts?* The law requires a tax on gifts such as jewelry, furs, or works of art. It is based on the fair market value of the item at the time the gift was presented. A rare 5 cent postage stamp, for example, is not worth 5 cents in the eyes of Internal Revenue. The current market value, above the $3000 exclusion, is taxable.

8. *Not All Gifts Less Than $10,000 Are Excluded.* There are some specific exceptions to the $10,000 exclusion. A life insurance policy that is given less than three years prior to the donor's death cannot be excluded, even if the annual premiums are less than $10,000. Gifts of "future interest," such as a trust fund for a child under twenty-one, cannot be excluded, even if its initial value was less than $10,000. You can get around that law by donating a "minor's trust," but all money accumulated until the child reaches legal age belongs to him or her.

The best advice is to give your money away wisely. You can save yourself and your beneficiaries quite a bit in taxes, but you also run the risk of depleting your resources in a short period of time.

A TAX BREAK FOR BENEFICIARIES WHO SELL INHERITED PROPERTY

A recent change in the tax laws will ease the already-high tax burden on inheritors. The revision serves as a tax break for those who sell inherited property that has markedly appreciated in value.

The Carryover Rule. This law was first passed by Congress in 1976. It allowed the government to tax heirs on the entire capital gain received from the sale of inherited property. The gain was assessed relative to the original owner's cost and the gain since, not what it was worth at the time of death. At the time the rule was approved, Congress felt the beneficiaries should pay taxes on the entire capital gain, not just on its value since the time of death.

Is It a Loophole? Lawmakers apparently thought so at the time it was passed. They felt the original purchaser and his or her heirs were getting away without paying taxes on property that would have been taxed had the original owner lived to sell it.

Be Aware of Congress' Capacity for Retreat. Most experts agree that Congress may modify these rules at some future date. If that happens, you can save yourself some hassles with the IRS by maintaining good records that post the original value of the property and its appreciation.

PROFESSIONAL HELP IN PREPARING YOUR TAX RETURN

If after all of this you can't figure out your income tax or potential deductions, don't feel alone. More and more Americans—over 30 percent of persons who file returns—are turning to professional tax preparers for help.

Who Are the Preparers? They range from Certified Public Accountants to established firms like H and R Block to rip-off artists who appear in January and vanish into thin air on April 15. The IRS also provides help, and will prepare returns at no charge for those who meet minimum standards: No more than $50,000 in income with no itemized deductions and without income averaging. There are also "enrolled agents" who pass an IRS-administered test, but be aware that there are no educational prerequisites for taking the exam.

Whom Should I Go to for Help? The IRS standards for preparing a return are described in the preceding paragraph. If you have a complex return full of capital gains, investment credits, and tax-shelter losses, a CPA would probably be your best bet. The fee is on an hourly basis and can range from $40 to $150 per hour. The Yellow Pages list CPAs, but you would be better off choosing one who is known and trusted by a friend or relative.

There exist uncertified public accountants who nonetheless have the educational background to prepare returns. Not all states offer certification, and the ones that do have stiff tests. A title of CPA is not a guarantee of good accounting ability.

A nationwide preparation firm like Block or Beneficial is good for someone with an uncomplicated tax return. Their fees are less than those of accountants, but the training of their employees is not as detailed as that of IRS preparers. Some of them may not be capable of representing you before the IRS, even though the law says they must.

A Final Note. Tax preparation has become a billion-dollar-a-year industry. It may be worth it for you to get more information or to pick up a tax guide and do it yourself.

TAX RIP-OFFS THAT COST YOU MONEY

Most Americans are honest about their incomes when they file with Internal Revenue. There are others, possibly millions, who lie to the IRS about how much they make. It is not done just once, but year after year.

How Much Is the IRS Losing? Some experts think that $250

to $400 billion per year in business transactions, mostly in cash, goes unreported, that $50 billion in taxes was unpaid, and that deductions were falsified to the tune of $18 billion. If these tax evaders were forced to pay up, say economists, the tax burden could be reduced as much as 10 percent.

Criticism of the IRS. There are those, particularly on Capitol Hill, who characterize the IRS as incompetent and inefficient in dealing with tax evaders. They feel that more and more Americans are feeling justified in falsifying their returns.

Underground Industries Springing Up. Cottage industries, which deal mostly in cash, are a primary source of frustration to the IRS. Narcotics, gambling on professional sports, pornography, and other such criminal activities have become billion-dollar industries. People working in legal enterprises often evade taxes the same way: waiters declare only a tiny portion of their tips, handymen are paid under the table, and merchants sell their products in flea markets, without records. Unless the IRS takes on the job of massive auditing, there is no way to stop this. Most of these people are probably basically law-abiding citizens who are tired of seeing the rich take advantage of special loopholes that significantly reduce their tax burden.

Why Doesn't IRS Crack Down? The IRS was not created to be in the collections business. Those on the inside claim the agency lacks the money and the manpower to enforce the tax laws which so may people break. In the meantime, the percentage of audits falls each year, while the number of unfinished investigations and uncollected accounts goes up. Its criminal investigations are under fire for their random selection and poor planning. In essence, the agency has found itself unable to cope with the underground economy. For the present, both Internal Revenue and its detractors hope that some tax reform as well as the Kemp-Roth tax plan will stop giving people the idea that they, as Americans, have a constitutional right to cheat the government.

11.
WILLS AND FUNERALS

YOU CAN'T TAKE IT WITH YOU—OR CAN YOU?

Estate taxes make some beneficiaries wish they had been left out of the will. Here are some things you can do to reduce your estate without sacrificing your financial well-being; to deal with the high cost of dying; and to avoid swindlers who take advantage of bereaved family members.

WHERE THERE'S A WILL, THERE'S A WAY

Drawing up a will is an unattractive task. It makes you aware of, among other things, your mortality. But if you are at all concerned about the people you leave behind, and leaving your estate to them, it is essential that a will be made.

Imagine going off to heaven and leaving your five-year-old daughter and son with no money to take care of themselves. Early consideration of these matters can save a great deal of hardship for your family later.

The process of drawing up a will goes by the name of "estate planning," which simply means that you legally establish who will receive your assets after your death. You decide exactly who your heirs are. Television and films may have given you the impression that only the rich have wills, which have been made in the oak-paneled drawing room of a mansion. But a will is important to anyone with property. Don't assume that your assets aren't worth anything. And remember: the government will get almost everything you have if you don't act first. The following 4 precautionary steps can save a lot of anguish for you and your heirs:

Step 1. Figure out how much you own and are worth. Add up your possessions, such as cash on hand, money in savings accounts, securities, property, retirement and Social Security benefits, and life insurance. Look around your home and determine the worth of your furniture, clothing, jewelry, hi-fi equipment, or other personal property. Most people have accumulated a lot more over the years than they think.

Step 2. Determine your debts. This is no fun, but it has to be done. Figure out what you owe to the bank on installment loans, charge accounts, and add up any outstanding bills.

Step 3. Subract what you *owe* from what you *own.*

Step 4. Write the will, telling your survivors how you want your assets to be distributed. It is important to see an attorney who can help you to execute a will legally. If you happen to own property or other investments jointly, the law usually allows the surviving party to inherit. Insurance policies are usually allocated to the previously designated beneficiaries.

WARNING: Without a will you run many risks. Your property may go to people you would prefer never saw it at all. It may pass on to young children who have no one designated to act as their guardian. A careless, spendthrift friend may inherit your assets. And finally, the federal or state governments may take more than their deserved share of your assets.

When you die without a will you are legally said to have died intestate. Under most state laws, this means that the court decides who will inherit your assets in this common order: spouse, children, parents, siblings, grandparents, cousins, the government itself.

Do you want these kinds of important decisions to be made by an indifferent judge in some courtroom? If not, execute a legal will that will put your money where it counts.

THE HIGH COST OF DYING AND WHAT YOU CAN DO ABOUT IT

Over the years, it has become more and more expensive to gracefully part with our loved ones. The funeral business is now nearly a $3-billion industry, and that figure continues to rise each year.

What can you do when unfortunate circumstances make it necessary for you to employ the services of a funeral home? The Federal Trade Commission has begun to pave the way for improvements in the funeral industry with a recent report criticizing some of the practices of American funeral homes.

This report can also serve as a guidebook for you when you enter a funeral home. When you first make your funeral arrangements, the best way to protect yourself is to have a calm, rational approach. But it is likely that you will not be in your best frame of mind. Perhaps, then, it is best to have some other party make the arrangements for you.

Watch out for untruthful claims and deceptive tactics. The FTC report revealed that each year the funeral industry makes at least forty million extra dollars by charging for items such as flowers and death notices that were provided by third parties.

Ask for an itemized listing of charges. Many funeral homes use what is called a lump-sum billing system that does not make clear what you are paying for and how much it costs. The FTC has even gone so far as to suggest that funeral homes should quote prices on the phone and advertise them in newspapers. This could allow the customer to compare prices and obtain the least expensive services.

Don't allow the kindly, understanding funeral parlor manager to take advantage of your emotional state. Many people have been pushed into buying expensive wreaths and caskets by unscrupulous funeral home owners.

The most important thing to remember is to *figure out what you can afford to spend on the funeral* services and attempt to *organize the fairest and most economical program possible.* The grief surrounding the death of a loved one will obviously put a tremendous strain on your emotions, but there is no reason why it has to do the same to your pocketbook.

COMMON SWINDLES USED ON PEOPLE WHO HAVE LOST A FAMILY MEMBER

It's hard to believe some scoundrel would try to bilk a woman whose husband just passed away. But there are con artists who specialize in this trap, and many times they are successful. If you ever lose a member of your family, here are 4 things to watch out for:

1. *The Insurance Swindle.* A rip-off artist contacts a recent widower and says he wants to pay off an insurance policy taken out by the deceased spouse. The only problem, he says, is that the policy ran out a few months ago. If you'll pay off the remainder of the policy, he continues, you'll get the insurance money. Don't be fooled. Why would your spouse take out a policy

and not tell you about it? Call the bluff of the "insurance salesman" and ask for the name and address of the home office.

2. *Debts Left by the Deceased.* Many crooks will attempt to convince widows that their spouse left unpaid loans. In most cases, the debt never existed, or it was paid off by the life insurance.

3. *COD Merchandise.* Sound like the movie *Paper Moon*? It happens. A crook will call on a widow and say that her spouse ordered certain merchandise. No, he didn't know he passed away. Don't be taken in. Of course he knows your husband died—he reads the obituaries every day. High-pressure tactics like these have been used to fleece widows for years.

4. *Don't Let Your Grief Cloud Your Vision.* The bunco artists I have described are preying on your despair. You are upset and depressed, and that's understandable. But don't let someone take advantage of you.

Part Two

FINANCIAL PLANNING

12.
YOUR INVESTMENTS

Your investments are the key to averting financial catastrophes and securing your retirement. But inflation is eating away at your money. What can you do about it? Are money market funds the best cushion against inflation? Could you be stretching your insurance dollar a little further? Keep reading to find the answers to these questions and more.

HOW TO HANDLE YOUR INVESTMENTS IN HARD TIMES

In a period of extreme fluctuations in practically every area of the economy, such as we are experiencing today, it is essential that you review your investments and begin making some changes. Here are 3 hints for doing this:

1. *Look at Interest Rates.* When interest rates begin to stagnate, it may be a sign to move out of short-term plans (13- and 26-week Treasury Bills) and into long-term bonds. Any slide in

interest rates may force bond prices up, but before that happens, you may be able to get high-yield bonds at discount rates.

2. *Observe What Other Investors Are Doing.* Many advisers and financial analysts are looking at the stock market and away from collectibles like gold and silver jewelry, coins and antiques. Many feel that collectibles have appreciated as much as they can, while an expected change in interest rates may push some stock issues up very high.

3. *Real Estate.* Despite a crunch in home building and home buying, many experts think real estate remains a terrific investment. Despite high mortgage rates, they say, the value of property will only increase. Until such time as mortgage rates come down, real estate provides a great tax shelter. In looking to the future in real estate, some investment counselors think vacation condominiums in trendy resort areas provide the best protection. One reason is that the people who can afford to purchase these condos are hardly affected by inflation or sky-high interest rates.

Keep in mind that interest rates have an impact on the rest of the economy. If you can time your investments to the rise or fall of interest rates, you may make out like a bandit.

HOW TO MAKE MORE MONEY ON YOUR SAVINGS ACCOUNT

There is no cut-and-dried way to tell exactly how much interest you can earn from a savings account. There are, however, 6 items you can verify to get an indication of which bank you should put your money into.

1. Check the passbook interest rate.

2. Find out when interest is compounded. Daily compounding will pay you more than annual compounding.

3. Find out what the annual percentage yield is. It is the actual number of dollars per $100 that your account will earn if left in the bank for a year.

4. If your account is day of deposit to day of withdrawal, you'll get interest on all of your money. Two unfavorable savings accounts are called lowest balance accounts (they pay interest on the lowest amount you had during the compounding period) and FIFO (first in, first out) accounts, which can deprive you of money you deposited early in the quarter.

5. Determine when the interest is actually paid. If interest payments are at the end of the quarter, you won't get a nickel if you close the account in the interim.

6. If you don't know what the interest payment rate is, you'll have no way of knowing if the correct amount of interest was credited to the account. If the bank won't tell you what it is or how to figure it out, go elsewhere.

13.
STOCKS AND BONDS

What do you do with your investment dollars? Is your money tied up in the stock market? In mutual funds? Is it safe? Millions of men and women play the stock market, but most aren't big winners. Is there any way you can increase your winnings?

In the following pages I'll discuss how to make money in a stagnant stock market, how to choose a broker, how to tell if your broker is cheating you. Do you know what a P/E ratio is? A neutral call? There's more to the stock and bond markets than simple buying and selling. This valuable information may help you make better decisions about your portfolio.

HOW TO DETERMINE THE VALUE OF STOCKS

When you approach the stock market, you are confronted by an array of thousands of companies that would like your investment dollars. The problem of course is selecting the ones that offer the best chances for profit, and determining their true value as opposed to mere claims.

Choosing the stocks that will bring you a good return is somewhat of a gamble—you never know for sure—until it happens—when and by what amount your stock will rise or fall.

The Greater Fool Theory. Even when you think your stock may be overpriced, it may go up. One shrewd stockbroker, Richard Wechter of L. F. Rothschild Unterberg Towbin, calls this type of occurrence the "greater fool theory." By that he means that even though the stock is overpriced, someone else will be willing to buy it at a still higher price. It's just one of those erratic factors that make the stock market so fascinating—and the constant flow of Dow Jones figures so necessary.

But what if you don't have years of experience buying and selling stocks? What if you don't have access to the kind of inside information you feel is necessary to do well in the market? Should you stay away from stocks?

Not necessarily. By using inductive reasoning—that is, by accumulating a wealth of facts and then coming to a general conclusion—you can begin to learn how a particular company operates.

In so doing, it is important to look at a company's *entire record*—not just their past year's earnings. A major corporation may, for instance, have an especially good year, and wind up with a level of earnings that is several million dollars above previous ones. Upon looking more closely at their profit and loss picture, however, you may find that previous years' earnings were just barely above the break-even point, or that the company's profit level has actually been going down, not up, over the long run.

In fact, there are at least 8 factors you should look at before deciding to buy a company's stock:

1. *Price/Earnings Ratio*. In brief, the price/earnings ratio is the price of the stock per share relative to the earnings of the company. Generally, this factor is valid only if earnings are staying the same or rising. There is some variation depending on the

type of industry. However, companies with low price/earnings ratios are usually those—such as tire or chemical manufacturers—which depend on growth in the economy for their own growth. High price/earnings ratio companies, on the other hand, have the ability to withstand economic fluctuations—and even prosper—in an economic downswing. The reason is that their products are always in high demand or are generally considered superior to others. So, when using this ratio, it's important to consider the industry.

2. *Book Value.* Our second estimate of the true worth of a stock is the book value of the company. This essentially means how many dollars the company would be worth if it were totally liquidated. However, sometimes the book value is not completely relevant in determining the value of a stock. Some companies, Marshall Field and SCM, for instance, traditionally sell their stocks at half book value. Thus, it is important for you to check into individual practices before you buy.

3. *Quality of the Management.* How well has the company been directed? Does it have a long history of shakeups in the upper echelons or has it been led by a more stable board with relatively little turnover? Is business conducted through a well-organized procedure that allows change to be introduced gradually or is its structure so rigid that it cannot readily adapt to changing circumstances? These are just a few of the questions you should ask yourself as you take a look at the inner workings of a corporation. It is entirely possible to have a company bring in an entirely new management team, dream up some wild scheme, earn a few extra million—then collapse when they can't maintain the momentum. On the other hand, a company that has followed a steady, almost predictable course for years can often withstand an occasional lapse in its earning power.

4. *Debt-to-Equity Ratio.* This is the amount of debt a company generally incurs in relation to its equity. Some companies have

no long-term debt and thus are given a low debt-to-equity ratio; others, conversely, seem to be always in debt. It is important to note, however, that debt in itself is not necessarily detrimental to a company's performance. The thing to look for is how well it is able to handle its debt.

5. *Cash on Hand.* A slightly different but related factor to the debt-to-equity ratio is a company's ability to pay current bills. Does it have enough cash and/or a good credit rating so it can raise the funds necessary to pay current bills? If not, why not?

6. *Inventory Turnover.* Another factor to look at is how quickly—or how slowly—a company is able to take in and sell its inventory. A low turnover may be indicative of inability to function well in economic downturns and/or adjust products to the marketplace. High turnover, on the other hand, is usually a good indication that a company knows how to take advantage of market trends and/or has a product that sells well despite economic fluctuations.

7. *Stage of Business Cycle.* Often, how well your chosen company's stock performs depends not so much on the company itself as it does on the stage of the business cycle. You can generally tell what stage the cycle is in by looking at the following factors:

- Has the Dow Jones Index been on a steady upturn (or downturn) for over eighteen months? (This is the usual extent of a business cycle.)
- What do the experts predict for the future?
- How do certain key indicators look: industrial inventory, balance of trade, Federal Reserve rate, and, of course, inflation?

8. *Return on Capital.* When a company puts money into a business, it expects to get some profit out of the investment. However, not all companies receive the same rate of return on their capital, and for many the rate of return may be far lower than you, as a stockholder, would prefer. Above all, if that rate

of return has been consistently below 2 percent for a period of several years, you are probably better off not investing in that company's stock.

HOW TO MAKE MONEY IN A STAGNANT STOCK MARKET

Even though most stocks trade in a very narrow range, there is an options strategy you can use which will result in a nice profit. The method is called a "neutral spread," and you will need a broker schooled in options trading because of the risk involved. The positives outweigh the negatives, especially in a recession market, and it's impossible to lose more than commission costs.

A neutral spread, also known as a "ratio bull spread" or "twofer," requires buying one call option on a stock and selling two call options on the same issue, both for the same period of time. A "call option" is the option to buy a stock at a certain price for a certain period of time. The trick is to find a stock whose options at the higher exercise price are trading at roughly half the premium of the option you're buying.

You will get more leverage from a spread than from an outright stock or option buy because little front money is needed. Most brokerages, however, have stiff margin requirements: $10,000 in equity on deposit with them in stock, Treasury Bills, or other fixed-income securities. A margin requirement is the amount of money which you must put up when buying a stock. This is generally true for any "naked call," an option on a stock you do not own. The collateral is used as a hedge against a possible exercise which would force you to deliver the stock you sold at a higher price.

With a neutral spread, you cover yourself by purchasing one

option, but not enough to offset the potential loss of both sell options.

If all of this sounds a little difficult to comprehend at first glance, don't be discouraged: many brokers have trouble with it. Make certain your broker is familiar with neutral spreads on naked calls and that you are both comfortable with that stock. To familiarize yourself with options trading, a book by Jarrott T. Miller called *Options Trading: Maximizing Profits, Minimizing Risks,* can be very helpful. Available from Contemporary Books, 180 N. Michigan Ave., Chicago, IL 60601.

HOW TO PREDICT WHAT THE STOCK MARKET WILL DO

Trying to figure out the stock market is a lot like trying to hit a pitcher with a 100-mile-an-hour fastball. You can get loads of advice, but once that baseball is flying toward your head, it's decision time.

Momentum and Trend. Many experts believe that momentum and trend are key in attempting to outguess the market. Since most stocks are destined to follow the market instead of leading it, you must spot the trend, time the reversal, and, most important, understand mass psychology. Sentiment will go a long way toward determining in what direction the market will go. The most popular of all technical-trend watchers is *The Granville Market Letter,* which caused the selling panic late in 1980.

Things the Amateur Can Find Useful. Technical jargon may be fine for the professionals, but it would probably make any amateur investor shake. However, some of the more popular methods for watching trends should be studied, even though they might not be the most sophisticated available. Much of this information can be ascertained just by reading the financial pages of the newspaper.

Some of the More Popular Indicators:

- *Advance/Decline Indicators.* Keep a running total, on a weekly basis, of advances versus declines. Simply subtract the number of stocks that went down from the number that were up. When declines begin to close in on the advances, it's time to bail out. The Dow Jones may still be high, but that index is not a reflection of all issues, just the more popular ones. And, say the experts, a rise in the Dow can't be sustained if other stocks are not keeping pace. A ten-day average of advances over declines may also be more helpful than a cumulative average.
- *Short-Interest Ratios.* Another trend analysts watch closely is the relationship between the amount of stock borrowed and sold short and the average daily volume. When the ratio over a month-long period reaches 1.5 (the sold-short amount being 1½ times greater than the volume) it is time to buy. This might seem paradoxical, but analysts see a short-term sellout as indication of future buys.
- *Overbought/Oversold Indicators.* This trend is measured over a ten-week period. If 70 percent of the stocks on the New York Exchange are selling above the Exchange average, the market is considered to be overbought, or ready for a fall. If fewer than 30 percent of the issues are selling above the average, it is a direct signal to buy.

Many large investors realize the unpredictability of the market, but they also say that that is what holds their interest over a long period of time. They may have more tools available than you, but a little work with the financial pages can be extremely helpful.

HOW TO READ THE STOCK QUOTATIONS

If you've ever tried to read a stock quotation from the newspaper, you know how tough it can be. To the beginner, it can look like hieroglyphics. But the information is important. Here's an explanation of the basic information in a stock quotation:

1. *52 Weeks High/Low.* This is the highest and lowest the stock has sold for in the preceding year.
2. *Div.* (dividend). This figure is the last dividend (per share) given by the company, either quarterly or semiannually. If there is a small letter next to the dividend amount, check the footnotes at the end of the quotation list.
3. *Yld %* (percentage of yield). This is the percentage relationship between the dividend and the price of the stock. A $1 dividend on a stock that sells for $20 is 5 percent.
4. *P/E Ratio* (price/earnings ratio). This is the twelve-month ratio between the current price and earnings. The P/E ratio is generally used to follow company trends.
5. *Sales 100s.* This is that day's volume (issues bought and sold) of that stock, in thousands. In the "Sales 100s" column, 262 means 262,000 shares of that stock were bought and sold on that day.
6. *High/Low.* This is the highest and lowest prices for the stock that particular day (as opposed to "52 Weeks High/Low"). A "u" next to the high number means the stock reached its highest level of the year. A "d" next to the low number means the stock reached its lowest point of the year.
7. *Close.* This is the price that stock was at at the end of the day's trading. 25½ means the stock closed at $25.50.
8. *Net Change.* How the price changed from yesterday's close. −2⅞ means the issue was down $2.875 that day.

Stock market quotations are to investors what box scores are to baseball fans. They give you the basic information. If, however, you want to know *why* the stock went down, or was heavily traded, or didn't pay a dividend that quarter, you'll have to do some research.

WHAT'S WRONG WITH THE P/E RATIO?

P/E ratios are tools used by many brokers to promote certain stocks. There are, however, some big doubts about their validity.

What Is a P/E? The price/earnings ratio is a simple concept to understand, a bit more complex to implement. It is, as mentioned, the price of a stock divided by its earnings per share. The theory behind a P/E is quite simple: investors should buy a stock when the P/E is low and sell it when the P/E rises.

Why Use It? Some analysts consider the P/E ratio a good way to judge a stock's popularity or to make comparisons of different issues in the same industry. Company officials see a higher earnings multiple as a way to issue more stock while making it more difficult for another company to buy them out.

What Are the Drawbacks? Stock predictions can be made worthless by any number of factors. One large problem with P/Es is that they are calculated by taking the most recent twelve months of earnings as reported by the company. Stock prices, however, reflect *future* considerations, so many analysts believe an estimate of anticipated earnings would be more valuable.

Another question mark regarding P/Es is that expectations do not always reflect a company's true potential. Skepticism about a particular company or industry can artificially drive down the P/E (which benefits the buyer more than the seller).

Modifying the P/E Ratio. There is an approach to the P/E that is very abstract. The ratio is arrived at by calculating the value of one dollar over a given period of time, taking into account a specific inflation rate. The price of a stock is then measured against the expected yield of low-risk instruments like Treasury Bills or money market funds. It is difficult, however, to predict inflation rates over any length of time.

The value of the P/E ratio is similar to any other method of analysis. The more investors who think it worthwhile, the more meaningful it becomes.

WHAT TO LOOK FOR IN A COMPANY'S ANNUAL REPORT

For stockholders or potential investors, an annual report is an important piece of information.

Companies will of course always try to make a report upbeat, but a discerning reader should look between the lines. Here are 3 clues to help you read financial reports:

1. *The Letter from the President.* The president's message summarizes how the company performed during the previous year. Weaknesses will be downplayed, so look for key words and phrases like "despite," "if this," or "except for." Strengths will be magnified, but don't be misled. Carefully note what, if any, expansion plans are in the works. If they are poorly timed, chances for increased earnings may be diminished.

2. *Financial Data.* This is crucial information which can be difficult to understand. Usually you will need more than one report as a means of comparison. "Accounts Receivable," the amount owed the company, and "Liabilities," what the company owes, are both very important. Also, check inventories against sales figures.

3. *Accountant's Statement.* This is usually at the end of the report, and it is simply a verification of the company's figures. If the accountant is questioning some of the data, you will see the words "Subject to." What follows can be very important and should be closely watched. It means the statement—or the numbers—cannot be considered totally reliable. Beware!

If you are already a stockholder, or are considering investing in a corporation, be sure to carefully read the annual or quarterly reports. Financial disclosure laws have made it easier to understand what's going on, but keep one thing in mind—the company writes the report, not an outside agency.

HOW TO READ A BALANCE SHEET—A GUIDE FOR BEGINNERS

If you are interested in buying stock, a balance sheet may be the only way you can figure out the company's financial situation. Here are 7 things you should do:

1. Get the most recent statement available. Business conditions can change, so a year-old balance sheet might not paint the true picture.

2. Read the auditor's opinion and make sure there are no unanswered questions. If there is no auditor's opinion to go along with the report, you may have reason to be suspicious.

3. Read the footnotes at the end of the report. The balance statement could be misleading if you don't look for any of the following: contingent liabilities, lease obligations, reserve account for contingencies, financial arrangements (to pay off debts), and capital assets. Items such as research and development, which require capital, could be included in "assets," even though they are intangible items.

4. Look for a large cash balance, especially where outstanding loans might be larger than the cash. This would be a danger signal.

5. Be aware that you don't know how much of the accounts receivable are simply bad debts which may never be collected.

6. Determine what type of inventory system the company uses. A large inventory could have a worthless cash value.

7. Understand the difference between net worth and profits. The net worth is made up of stockholders' money and what the company actually earned (or lost). If the deficit is larger than the profit, especially for two years running, the company could be in trouble.

COMMODITIES TRADING: BIG WINNERS AND BIG LOSERS

The desire for a quick killing has led many investors down the speculative road, of which commodities trading is a popular side road. Many investors like the fast pace, the high leverage, and the chance to make big money in a hurry. Be forewarned, however, that commodities are not for the timid. Although many people have retired on their winnings, even more have lost their shirts—but not the bug.

What Are Commodities? Commodities are items that trade at the present for their future value. Ten exchanges in the United States currently trade in futures in corn, soybeans, wheat, and other agricultural products or gold, silver, Treasury Bills, and foreign currencies.

How Are They Traded? Commodities are traded in a manner similar to stock options. You can buy a contract in which you agree to buy a fixed amount of that commodity at a specific future date. Or, you can sell a contract by agreeing to deliver that item at a fixed date. The total worth of the contract can be enormous, but you generally need only 10 percent of the cash up front.

What Should Your Strategy Be? Unless you have a specific need for a product, you almost always sell it off before the contract expires—either because you've made as much money as you think you can or because you don't want to risk losing any more than you already have. You should never let the contract reach a point where you would be obligated, for example, to accept delivery of 10,000 bushels of wheat.

7 Rules to Follow:

1. Put up only money that you can afford to lose and are prepared to lose. You must also decide whether you will manage your own fund or have a broker do it for you. The cash needed to start on your own is steep—more than $10,000. A broker will want considerably less.

2. Study the markets before getting involved. You must understand, prior to trading, how outside factors can affect commodities futures. For example, the state of the economy in Europe will have a direct effect on certain farm commodities, and that can spill over into the silver and gold markets. Publications like *The Wall Street Journal* print daily commodity reports as well as government reports you will want to become familiar with: Crop forecasts, for example.

3. Stay with commodities you have some experience with on another level, possibly in your line of work. If you're an East Coast business executive, you may know very little about agricultural products, although you are well versed in gold and silver. Stick with what you know.

4. Develop an individual trading strategy. Decide beforehand how long you want your money tied up, what kind of a profit you're willing to settle for, and how much you can afford to lose before ending a contract. Do not change your strategy in midstream. There are a number of schools of thought when it comes

to commodities trading, but many successful investors use a combination of market supply and demand and current market performance. If you make your trades on paper with play money, you can get a good feel for the market.

5. Never spend more than 25 percent of your "available" money. This will cushion you against a downturn which could necessitate your adding more margin money.

6. Don't spread yourself too thin. If you only have enough time to get deeply involved in one commodity, don't diversify. That will only confuse the issue.

7. Keep your eyes and ears open. The commodities market is so volatile that you must always keep abreast of the situation. A steady flow of information, from either your broker or outside sources, will be extremely helpful.

Veteran speculators warn about catching commodities fever, and insist that nothing fuels it like success. Watch your step. It is a sad fact that some 80 percent of small traders in commodities futures contracts lose money. The main reason is that they behave as though they were betting in a pool hall and forget basic strategy.

There are few forms of speculation that provide the possibility of such huge gains in so short a time, but the rule that small traders tend to ignore is that they should use as little initial capital as possible. Too many traders limit their chances of success by being fully invested.

Of course, leverage in these matters is essential. But it is also very important to have sufficient backup funds to cover the price volatility that can wipe out thinly margined positions with a simple swing back and forth in the space of a minute or an hour. Commodity traders should put up only as much as 5 percent of the value of the contract (which is all that the exchanges and brokers require anyway).

Another problem that too many traders have is an unwarranted fear of selling too short. The fallacy that you shouldn't sell something you don't own is taken advantage of by professional traders. They wait for the small speculators to sell into the market, then wait for the thinly margined investors to panic and drop their contracts when their brokers advise it. This is often a case whereby the investors are just too stubborn to admit they are wrong. So, instead of wisely taking losses, they wait around and get smeared. It doesn't cost you anything to place stop-loss orders when you take a position, and it is the only sure way to keep your losses down to a bare minimum. In short (to make a pun), don't let greed put you in the red!

THE ABCS OF OPTIONS

Woody Hayes, former coach of the Ohio State Buckeyes, often grumbled that only three things can happen when you throw a pass—and two of them are bad. The same can be said for stock options. It's an investment which is risky, but which can be very profitable.

What Is an Option? An option gives you the right to buy shares of stock for a prescribed length of time, at which time the option expires. This "unbalanced contract," for which the buyer pays a premium, gives him or her the flexibility to decide whether or not to fulfill the obligation.

How Does an Option Contract Work? An option contract specifies the transfer of one option (100 shares) of that stock, and can be exercised until it expires, usually the third Saturday of any month less than one year away. The exercise price can be lower than the current market price (out of the money), equal to it (on the money), or higher than it (in the money).

How Price Is Determined. Two factors go into the pricing of an option:

1. Its underlying value: the market price of the stock and the expectations of its value in the future.

2. Time value: the longer the option, the higher the price. Quite simply, the longer you have to exercise the option, the better chance it has of moving up or recovering from a fall.

Where to Look for Help. Market services such as *Daily Graphs/ Stock Option Guide* or *The Option Strategist* develop values of particular options based on a large number of factors. These publications are utilized by brokers to check against their own judgment of premium prices. No investor wants to overpay.

Placing Limit Orders. Once you have settled on a price, contact your broker and tell him or her to put a limit order on that option. You may pay less than the market, especially if orders are piled up ahead of you. If, however, that option is unavailable at that price, you have no purchase. Experts agree, though, that placing limit orders lessens the risk.

4 Types of Options: There are 4 possibilities for you to consider:

1. Buy a call: this option allows you to purchase 100 shares in hopes the stock will rise.

2. Write a put: this is an obligation to purchase 100 shares at a price and collect the premium. The speculator, however, has the upper hand in this action. Why? Because he can collect his premium—or hold the share for potential future gain.

3. Buy a put: the privilege of selling 100 shares.

4. Write a call: the obligation to sell the shares.

These actions reward the speculator for his added risk. Most experts agree that the amateur should avoid the more speculative actions. One way to reduce risk is to manipulate the narrowing or widening of the price differentials by making two calls on the same security.

Covered Writing. This is also a risk-avoidance measure, accomplished by writing a call, or obligating yourself to sell. The difference in this case is that you are writing calls on stock you already own. It serves the purposes of providing some additional income and a measure of protection for your stock against a downturn equal to the premium. In covered writing, work with a stock you would have bought anyway, and make sure the quoted premium is worth at least 10 percent of the market price.

NEUTRAL CALLS: WINDFALL OR DOWNFALL?

Large jumps or falls in the stock market can give anyone ulcers. Some speculators, however, are making a volatile market and economic apprehension work for them in the area of options trading. The neutral call has become the new wave for speculators.

How It Works. A neutral, or "straddle," is a gamble of the longest shot, but its popularity is increasing among investors who are tired of trying to outguess the market. In making a neutral call, you don't care whether the stock goes up or down, as long as it goes. The only time you're a loser is when it remains steady through the period when you must exercise your options.

Puts, Calls, Neutrals. If you don't straddle, you either buy a call (buy the stock if you exercise the option) or write a put (sell the shares if you exercise the option). With a neutral call, you do both on the same stock, spit into the wind, and see where it falls. The secret is to choose an issue that has a chance of moving rapidly, either up or down the ladder. If the stock goes up, the call rises and the put falls accordingly. The same holds true for an issue that declines. Put goes up, call goes down.

Example: XYZ Corporation stock traded within a range of $60

to $135 a share for the previous quarter, and is now selling at $100. The wide divergence indicates it might be a good bet for a neutral call. The call is 5, meaning 100 shares (one option) will cost you $500. The put is 4, so add another $400. Total investment, $1000 including commissions (another $50 to $100). The options expire in one month. In that month, the stock must drop to $90 or rise to $115 for you to make a profit using the "straddle-strategy" noted above.

Are Options Profitable? The answer is unquestionably no. So why do it? There is a chance, every once in a while, that you'll come out a big winner. The secret to options is knowing when to get out and when to stay in. Either cut your losses or attempt to double your money.

A WORD TO THE WISE

Any sort of options trading is obviously highly speculative. The opportunity to win big is what drives many people, but if you don't have a lot of capital to lose, you should forget the whole thing.

WHAT YOU SHOULD KNOW BEFORE YOU BUY YOUR FIRST STOCK OR BOND

The first decision of what to invest your money in depends on how you feel about the government and inflation. If you think government and inflation deficits will get worse, don't bother to invest in stocks or most bonds. If you're optimistic, then decide whether you want current income or a long-term growth.

Either way, if you already have your available money invested in a money market fund with high interest rates, keep about 50 percent of it there. It will still earn a good return with little risk. Twenty percent of what you have ought to go into a common-stock mutual fund that stresses long-term asset growth. Many of these funds have a lot of cash they are just beginning to invest in the market. With the remaining 30 percent of your available funds you can experiment in choosing individual stocks. Major companies usually do well during recessions and are more stable. Cyclical stocks in such industries are often bargains. A third kind of stock involves companies in financial services areas whose earnings respond well to lower interest rates.

You are looking for the effect economic and social trends will have on an industry or on a company. But be rational and analyze the company in which you want to invest.

The next decision in buying stock is which stockbroker to hire. Most are uninterested in the modest customer. In fact, most of a broker's business is done by only 20 percent of the customers. Representatives are brokerage firm salesmen; basically, they are order takers. A "rep" rarely has any new or unusual information, because his or her information has usually come from the firm's research department, and the big mutual funds and pension funds have usually informed the firm. There is little capital appreciation left in the stock by the time you hear of it. This is why 50 percent of a broker's transaction is unsolicited, which means dictated by the customer.

Major national brokerages (also known as wire houses) offer a wider range of financial services than the smaller firms. These major houses offer stock and bond mutual funds, money market funds, and sometimes even real estate syndications. But they tend to be impersonal. The smaller firms are good for beginners with a bit of money to invest because they'll give him or her more attention.

Discount brokers, or transaction specialists, are about half the cost of the others, but they offer none of the services. There have been rumors that transaction specialists are more disorganized and not to be trusted, but in truth they are probably as good as anyone else.

When you choose a firm, first meet with the branch manager. He or she will recommend a representative with common tastes in investment objectives, such as long- or short-term growth and performance, or current income.

If you are a beginner, it is advisable not to open a *margin account.* Trading on margin is trading on borrowed money. You can borrow 50 percent of the cost of your trade from your broker, who in turn borrows from a bank. This makes for about 12 percent interest charged to you. You can buy twice as many stocks, but it is then twice as risky, and if the stocks drop you have to pay the difference to maintain the collateral position on the loan.

A *cash account* saves you the time of exchanging checks with your broker since you have cash on deposit. This cash earns no interest, however. Some firms sell and manage money market funds as storage for your funds, with interest.

If for some reason you don't trust your broker, you can open another account and compare notes. It's an expensive precaution but gives you two professional opinions. In the long run, you must trust someone. You've known from the beginning that stocks and bonds are a gamble.

Newsletters, put out by reporting services and companies themselves, can give you specific information on company histories and recent patterns of stock movement and company growth. The amount and variety of advice can be overwhelming, as everyone has different recommendations.

Stocks and bonds can be an excellent investment and you can learn a lot along the way. They will teach you about this country's economy and the international economy, as well as the social factors that influence them. And they will teach you how to make your nest egg grow. Just be analytical and imaginative and, with some luck, you will enjoy yourself and the profits that will come from the experience.

---

10 RULES TO FOLLOW WHEN DOING BUSINESS WITH YOUR STOCKBROKER

There is no reason why you should allow your stockbroker to do anything he or she feels like with your money. You can watch a small fortune disappear this way. There are 10 basic rules that can help you keep your broker in check and keep a better eye on your money:

1. Keep informed of your rights and let your broker know you are knowledgeable.

2. Set down the ground rules before you have extensive dealings with your broker. For example, if you prefer that he not speculate with your money without checking with you first, let him know. Many people have lost money because their brokers went haywire with speculative stocks that failed.

3. If you feel that your broker has somehow misrepresented your interests, don't immediately run to the Securities and Exchange Commission. Go directly to your broker and tell *him* your grievances, first.

4. Perhaps the broker can solve the problem immediately. If not, it might be necessary as a next resort to speak to the branch manager or compliance officer of his or her firm.

5. If the broker *is* at fault, try to get the firm to reimburse you or, alternatively, get the broker to reimburse you.

6. If that's a dead end, contact the Security and Exchange Commission, 500 N. Capitol St., Washington, D.C. 20549. They

will either begin an investigation or contact the firm for follow-up.

7. Send a carbon copy of your complaint to the exchange that your broker belongs to.

8. Follow up the letter to the exchange. They will normally contact the offending broker and request an explanation.

9. It is possible that you will not be satisfied with your broker's explanation, and will want to pursue the matter further. Considering how high court costs can be, you might want to first try arbitration. The New York Stock Exchange, for example, examines cases at a fraction of what it might cost to take the matter to court.

10. Finally, if the matter necessitates litigation, shop around for good lawyers in this field and always attempt to get the best advice you can. Try to find a lawyer who has been involved in similar cases successfully.

SHOULD YOU BE USING A DISCOUNT BROKERAGE HOUSE?

You've seen the ads for discount brokerage houses. They talk about big savings on commissions, which is great—if you know what you're doing.

A discount house is not your typical brokerage. It does not as a rule offer advice or manage your portfolio. What it will do, however, is execute any buy or sell order for a considerably smaller fee (depending on the size of the order) than a regular brokerage firm.

You should consider opening an account with a discounter if:

1. You have the time and energy to manage your own portfolio.

2. You have the research materials necessary to make decisions or you have your own investment counselor.

3. You have a small number of issues that you no longer want—stock you acquired as a gift, for example.

4. You need to make a large transaction to raise capital. The discounts on large orders can be substantial.

If you are considering switching your present account to a discount broker, there are 3 things to consider:

1. Will your orders be executed immediately after you tell the broker?

2. Does the firm have enough people on the floor of the exchange to execute your buy or sell order promptly and efficiently?

3. Does the firm charge an annual service fee to discourage small orders?

You can save as much as 80 percent on commissions by using a discount house—provided the order is large enough and you don't need the services offered by typical brokers.

A BASIC GUIDE TO MUTUAL FUNDS

In his first State of the Economy address, President Reagan held up an American dollar in one hand and a small handful of coins in the other to illustrate the decreasing value of our currency.

This perhaps exaggerated demonstration points out a concern among most Americans about the value of their money. More and more people are seeking and finding alternative ways to invest their money. One such alternative is the mutual fund.

What Are Mutual Funds? Mutual funds are basically a pooling of several investors' money to be invested in some prescribed way. They are often designed for the small investor who would find it too costly to employ someone to manage his or her money professionally. They are usually considered ideal by investors who do not have a great deal of time to spend on their investments. Small investors usually have other jobs, making it difficult for them to keep informed about the latest market developments.

How They Work. Generally you invest your money in the common pool and pay for the total management of the fund, usually about one-half of 1 percent of the fund's assets. If the fund is sold to a broker or salesman, there may be a sales charge of anywhere between 1 and 8 percent. Many funds are also sold by direct marketing.

Many funds do not do very well, but for the most part they perform as well, if not better, than other managed accounts. According to a recent issue of *American Money Reporter,* top money funds yield well over 11.25 percent.

Which Mutual Fund Should You Choose? This depends largely on what you want to get out of it. An investor who has a pretty good income and who can afford to take some risk is probably more interested in long-term investment with higher yields.

Specialized Funds. You may have special areas of interest that you would like to invest in. There are funds that search out and invest in small, aggressive companies, for example. There are option funds that try to buffer you from the unpredictable swings of the market. There are internationally oriented funds and precious metal funds. Cautious investors can place their money in tax-exempt-bond funds such as the Federated Tax-Free Income Fund. Money market funds are popular because of their liquidity and safety. They are often invested in Treasury Bonds, certificates of deposit, commercial paper, and other short-term paper. Bond funds, such as the Fund for U.S. Government Securities, offer a long-term, high-yield investment for the conservative investor.

Starting Your Investment in Mutual Funds:

1. Find out more about the fund or funds you are interested in. One source of information is the Investment Company Institute, 1775 K St. NW, Washington, D.C., (202)293-7700.

2. Once you have found the funds that appear to use the strat-

egies you like, check into their performance statistics. A good source is the Wiesenberger Investment Companies Service, 1633 Broadway, New York, NY, (212)977-7453.

3. After you have narrowed down your list, get the prospectuses of the funds you like. Read them over carefully to see how each company operates and whether you can or wish to invest in it.

4. After you have invested in the fund, read the quarterly and annual reports for changes in management and fund objectives.

SOME BASIC TRAINING ABOUT THOSE MONEY MARKET FUNDS

A passbook savings account is a poor hedge against inflation. Long-term certificates provide higher yields, but you risk paying a penalty if you ever need to withdraw your money. With these things in mind, you may want to consider money market funds.

What Is a Money Market Fund? A money market fund is an investment plan whereby you, along with other investors, provide a pool of money which is used to purchase a wide range of short-term securities such as Treasury Bills or bank certificates of deposit. Your investment can be as little as $1000.

Are There Penalties for Withdrawals Before Maturity? No. You can get your cash whenever you need it, and most funds provide free check-writing services.

Are Money Market Funds High-Risk Investments? No. There is no reason why your money would be any safer in a bank or other financial institution, as long as you deal with a reputable fund. Read the fund's prospectus and make sure it deals in high-grade securities.

Are There Any Organizations That Offer Objective Information on Money Market Funds? A publication by William E. Donoghue called the *Money Market Fund* lists most available funds and in what they invest. Before you make any transaction, however, get a prospectus and study it carefully.

Don't let your lack of knowledge about them prevent you from considering money market funds. If you are content to let your money sit in a savings account and collect interest that is not much more than the inflation rate, you might as well give your money away on the street.

---

7 THINGS YOU SHOULD KNOW ABOUT MONEY MARKET FUNDS

With the Federal Reserve Board insisting that interest rates will remain constant through most of 1984, you can expect more cash to be invested in money market mutual funds. Remember:

1. *Money Market Funds Are a Good Investment.* Because of the inflationary pressures, a number of experts say that this is the right time to get into money market funds.

2. *Money Market Funds Offer the Most Liquidity.* They are a fine way to capitalize on the money rate game. You can get out at any time, without the penalty, and the initial investment is $1000 or less.

3. *Other Investments Offer High Yields, But Withdrawal Is Difficult.* A six-month savings certificate has a high yield, but you can lose at least ninety days of interest if you cash in early. A six-month Eurodollar deposit is just $1000, but if you choose to sell it back prior to maturity, you risk a loss if interest rates go down.

4. *You Must Pick a Money Market Fund Carefully.* The choice of a fund usually comes down to the range of services offered:

check writing, phone withdrawals, and the opportunity to make exchanges with other funds written by the same management company. All funds put their money into the same short-term investments: Treasury Bills, bank certificates of deposit, commercial paper, and bankers' acceptances.

5. *Compare Long-Term Yields.* This is one method you can use in deciding on a money market fund. Quotes usually offer a reflection of performance over the past few days. A long-term figure will help you determine stability.

6. *Work With Your Broker.* If you are a serious investor, you can save yourself some hefty transfer fees by investing in a fund offered by your broker.

7. *You Must Look for Information.* William E. Donoghue has been keeping close tabs on money market funds for almost 8 years and is considered by many to have the most insight. He tracks the yields of money market funds and probably has the most complete list available. His weekly publication, *Donoghue's Money Fund Report* is available by writing Box 641, Holliston, MA 01746. A directory describing each fund and its services is also available at a reasonable cost.

IS YOUR BROKER CHEATING YOU? IF SO, WHAT YOU CAN DO

You pay your broker a commission. You place your trust in him or her. What if this trust is betrayed?

Don't stand for it. There are a number of ways you can remedy the situation, from calling his or her supervisors to legal recourse. And the increasingly popular stock exchange arbitration often settles disputes outside of court. The New York Stock Exchange initiated arbitration for claims under $2500, and the Securities and Exchange Commission has ruled that investors can file for arbitration regardless of the clauses in their customer agreement. A boon for investors? Maybe. A hassle for brokers? Probably.

Here are 6 examples of major complaints that are filed against brokers:

1. Ignoring buy and sell instructions. You want 100 shares of ABC Corporation but your broker buys 150 shares of ABE. Or, you phone in a sell order at ten in the morning and she places it at two that afternoon, after the issue has plunged.

2. Failing to adhere to the client's stated objective. You're an elderly widow on a fixed income and he buys speculative issues in energy and casinos.

3. Making unauthorized transactions without the client's knowledge or consent.

4. Giving advice based on fictitious or misleading information.

5. Encouraging unnecessary transactions for the sole purpose of beefing up commissions. This is known in the trade as churning.

6. Hyping options without explaining the inherent risks to the investor.

Many small- and medium-sized investors handle their investments themselves, but those with large portfolios usually can't keep abreast of all of the current developments without the help of a broker. When something goes wrong, especially if it's a routine mistake (not placing an order on schedule) you may not be able to expect help from the brokerage. At that point, you still have 3 choices, 2 cheap, 1 extremely expensive:

1. A formal, written complaint to the SEC and the exchange on which the stock trades.

2. Formal arbitration of your claim against the broker, using the standard operating procedure employed by all exchanges.

3. A lawsuit.

Except for the written complaint, each action has its price. There are no guarantees of the success of a lawsuit, a procedure which could set you back a few thousand dollars. Arbitration costs less (about $400), but there is still no guarantee of satisfaction. Small-claim arbitration (claims of less than $2500) cost just $15, but you risk a potential counterclaim by the brokerage house.

Deciding What to Do. Some cases are so clear-cut (you order a buy, the broker writes sell on the invoice) that the brokerage house will almost always credit your account, even at the branch office level. No firm wants to take a chance of losing in court.

Unfortunately, most cases, especially those involving "misinformation" or churning, are very difficult to prove. Detailed records, which might be hard to acquire, are of great importance. Talk with your broker first and work your way up the ladder until you receive satisfaction—the branch manager, then someone at corporate headquarters. (Allow the branch manager five days to take action, two weeks for someone at upper management level.)

If you must write a formal letter, be extremely cautious. Many investors tan their own hide by exaggerating the amount of money they lost, with the intent of squeezing the broker. Such an attack, if discovered by your broker, will result in the case being turned over to the legal department.

After you have gone as far as you can, with no success, write a formal letter of complaint to the SEC's Office of Consumer Affairs, 500 N. Capitol St., Washington, D.C. 20540. Send copies, along with a covering letter, to the branch manager of the brokerage firm, the president of the firm, and the appropriate stock exchange. Give the facts in detail: the name of the broker, a summary of your charges, and, most important, an estimate of the damages. If your complaint involves allegations of dishonesty, include a list of the suspect transactions. In dollar figures, show exactly how your account stands with and without those transactions. Give the SEC two to three weeks to respond, and six weeks thereafter for the broker. If the brokerage still refuses to take action, it's time to get a lawyer, either for arbitration or court action.

Arbitration. Small-claims arbitration is handled by the arbitration director of the stock exchange involved. Submit your claim and wait no more than twenty days for the brokerage house to respond. The decision, normally reached without a hearing, takes another eight weeks.

If a hearing is requested by yourself or the arbitrator, it is usually held in a city where a stock exchange is located. It is a semiformal process, with sworn testimony and the oppportunity for both sides to present their case. A normal hearing takes two to three hours to complete, three or four months for a decision.

In cases where the dollar value is higher than $2500, a panel of three to five arbitrators is used. The hearing procedure is more complex, and it takes almost twice as long to reach a decision.

Lawsuits. A lawsuit should be your last resort, after everything else has failed. The one advantage of a lawsuit over arbitration is that a jury may be more inclined in your favor than a stock exchange arbitrator, so your chances of winning may be better.

Police Your Broker. The best way to avoid any of these contingencies is to keep a close eye on your broker. He or she may be taking your account for granted and is becoming sloppy and indifferent. Be a demanding client. After all, it's your money.

14. REAL ESTATE

Those who can afford it can beat inflation and make money through land purchases. Land alone in some exclusive parts of the country is selling for upwards of $100,000 an acre—and this is without any existing structure on it. For those in the lower income brackets, increasing real estate prices have changed every rule that used to apply to home buying.

It used to be that buying a home was considered prudent only if the payments did not exceed 25 percent of the household income. Now, however, this is often impossible. Young couples are finding it necessary to borrow from relatives or to get mortgages with longer payment schedules. It is estimated that more than two-thirds of all home buyers are now families with two wage earners.

10 THINGS YOU SHOULD KNOW IF YOU WANT TO INVEST IN LAND

Land can be a great investment if you know what you're doing. Here are 10 things you should consider before buying any piece of property:

1. *Study.* Bone up on land as an investment and get professional advice. There are many easy-to-understand guides for amateur investors. Consult your local librarian or bookseller.

2. *Understand the Zoning Laws.* The money you make on the resale of property will largely depend on its potential uses for the buyers. In a depressed housing market, land zoned strictly for residences won't bring as much as land zoned for industry.

3. *Be Well Versed About the Area.* Find out things such as the area's growth rate, property values of comparable land, and the climate for reselling. Local government officials, realtors, even neighbors, can help you get a grip on the subject.

4. *Could the Property Sell As Is?* In other words, how much money would you have to spend on improvement to sell the property for a good profit? If you have to drill a well or install phone lines to make it more attractive, your profit will obviously be reduced.

5. *Can the Land Earn Money While the Value Appreciates?* If you can rent the land to campers, plant crops, or find another use for the property in the time before you sell, you will increase your profit.

6. *Sell the Least Valuable Parcels First.* The most desirable land will always increase in value more quickly. Hold on to those parcels.

7. *Watch Out for Distress Sales.* You may indeed get a bargain if a landowner must sell out, but it could also be used as a cover for worthless property. Scrutinize any distress purchase.

8. *Understand How Economic Developments Affect the Value of the Property.* If your land is intended for a resort, let's say, and the price of gasoline goes through the roof, you may have a hard time selling it.

9. *Arrange the Best Financing Available.* Any mortgage you can pass on to the next owner is an advantage.

10. *Avoid High-Pressure Promotions.* If a piece of property is ridiculously cheap, be more skeptical than normal. There may be a reason why a piece of land is unwanted. Find out why.

15.
COMPANY BENEFITS

---

13 QUESTIONS YOU SHOULD ASK ABOUT YOUR COMPANY'S BENEFIT PLAN

With inflation over the past years, fringe benefits, a once overlooked but very valuable asset, are being watched more closely.

There is a distinct difference between a "good" benefit plan and a "bad" one. Health and disability benefits are virtually universal these days, but one area getting more recognition is in profit-sharing and "thrift" plans. Let's examine those first.

1. *How Much Can I Contribute to a Profit-Sharing Plan?* Most of these plans allow employees to contribute as much as 6 percent of their annual income. Your contributions, which are tax free, earn interest and dividends on a tax-deferred basis.

2. *How Much Does the Company Contribute?* A company usually matches 50 cents on the dollar, although some firms, oil companies, for example, will match dollar for dollar. You immediately receive at least a 50 percent return on your investment, and a conservatively managed fund will yield a remarkable return. One benefit expert estimates that a long-time employee can retire with almost twice his or her final annual salary. A straight profit-

sharing plan, one that doesn't require employee contributions, should contribute 2 to 3 percent of each employee's salary.

3. *When Should I Withdraw the Money?* Your best move, if possible, is to leave the money alone until you retire. At that point you can treat the entire package as a capital gain and cut the tax rate appreciably in several different ways. Since the interest and dividends are tax deferred, one tax expert says, you can average it out over ten years and pay as little as 15 to 18 percent. You also have the option of putting your money into an Individual Retirement Account (IRA) and letting it earn more.

4. *How Easy Are Withdrawals?* Since companies are also taxed when you withdraw any money, there are some obstacles set forth to make that choice difficult to exercise. There are no financial penalties, although many companies will require you to stop contributions from three to six months after a withdrawal. In the long run, you will lose money this way, since the company isn't obligated to contribute if you don't. A more liberal plan will examine each individual's case and will permit withdrawals for those who can demonstrate hardship. You will, of course, have to pay regular income tax on any withdrawal—although your contribution does not apply.

5. *What Are the Investment Choices?* A progressively managed plan allows you a number of investment choices. The company's contributions are usually invested in company stock. The remaining balance, including your contribution, can be invested in a diversified or fixed-income portfolio. Most plans have a reputation for cautiousness, although some are now moving into high-yield, money market issues because of the high interest rates. A relatively new item, guaranteed income contract (GIC), is being recommended by investment specialists. The GIC is a fixed-income fund managed by an insurance company. If the interest rate rises, your earnings will follow suit. The guarantee comes into play should interest rates fall. The floor is normally around

8 percent, and it's a good way to lock in a return if the bottom falls out of the economy. The only drawback to a GIC, however, is that if interest rates rise, only new contributions are assessed the higher rate of return. Old money stays at the lower level.

6. *How Is the Plan Vested?* The settlement of a good plan is usually 100 percent over five years. This is known as "cliff" vesting because of the way it appears on a graph. A "class-year" vesting plan penalizes employees who have longer service with the company. In this type of settlement, it normally takes two years for the plan to vest. It has the effect of making it unattractive for a middle-level employee to leave, because he or she forfeits the company contributions from the unvested years when his or her salary was at its highest.

7. *What Is the Cost of Health and Disability Coverage?* A good plan shouldn't cost you a nickel in premiums. As with most insurance policies, there is a deductible requirement. More on that to follow.

8. *What Should It Cover?* A good plan should offer full coverage for a three-week hospital stay, diagnostic tests in a hospital, mental health care, extended-care facilities, eye care, dental care, and postretirement needs. A few things to know in addition: Some plans do not cover diagnostic work that requires hospital admission. The reason is that most of this testing can be done on an outpatient basis. Many dental plans will not pay for extensive work like crowns, bridgework, or orthodontia for your children. Mental health coverage is also very tenuous in many places. If you work in a city that has what one expert calls "creative business" (New York or Los Angeles are prime examples), you'll be lucky to get any psychiatric coverage. Also, most plans pay only 50 percent of psychiatric costs rather than the traditional 80 percent. The cost of counseling is generally fixed, regardless of income, which makes it difficult for some people.

9. *What Should the Deductible Be?* The deductible require-

ment, the initial cost to you before the plan begins to pay, should be no more than $250 for major medical ($500 per family) and $50 and $150 for dental.

10. *How Much Does It Pay?* Most medical plans, aside from mental health plans, are very uniform, and pay 80 percent of major medical and dental and 20 percent of mental health.

11. *Is There a Limit to My Costs?* Most good plans have a "stop-loss" feature. Your costs end after the first $1000, regardless of the final bill. In the case of catastrophic illness, there is no need to tell you how beneficial that can be.

12. *How Much Should It Pay for Short-term Disability?* For the first six months of a short-term illness, a 100 percent salary continuation is granted, depending on length of service; usually, two weeks for every year with the company. This can provide a gap in pay for newer employees, although many companies offer a medium-term plan of 50 percent of salary.

13. *What About Long-term Illness?* After six months, a good disability plan will pay 50 to 60 percent of your salary, and you will still receive your benefits from Social Security.

Remember, a job is always worth more than its base pay. With costs rising, especially medical costs, benefits are not something to be taken for granted.

16. YOUR OWN BUSINESS

HOW TO SUCCEED WITH THE GOVERNMENT'S HELP

Believe it or not, the federal and state governments are behind small businesses. Besides the ugly regulations, taxes, permits, and restrictions they impose on you, there are actually programs that are designed to help your business prosper.

One such program is sponsored by the Small Business Administration and makes millions of dollars available in the form of loans and grants. It is quite possible that you qualify for one of them.

There are certain requirements for you to qualify. There are also restrictions on how the money may be used once received. The best thing to do is to contact the SBA and ask for details. The SBA is there to help you.

The SBA will lend you money, at a low interest rate, so you will have the capital to start your business. You can borrow money from them to build a plant, for expansion, equipment, supplies, and raw materials.

How Much Can the Government Do? Under the SBA is an organization called Small Business Investment Companies. They are entitled to make long-term loans to developing businesses, and are regulated and overseen by the SBA. This group of companies will lend you anywhere from $25,000 to $5 million to start your new business, and will also provide you with advice and guidance. All small entrepreneurs are well advised to contact this office. Their headquarters' address is: Small Business Administration, 1030 15th St. N.W., Washington, D.C. 20417. Or check the phone book in your area to see if there's a local SBA chapter.

Expanding Your Business. You might wonder whether the SBA would stop helping you once you become a large business. A small business is defined as one employing fewer than 250 employees. Anything else is considered large.

If you run a wholesale operation and your annual sales do not exceed $5 million, you are considered a small business. Retail and service operations are deemed small businesses if they take in less than a million dollars each year.

If your business falls under one of these categories, then you are eligible for government aid for expansion.

SBA Can Guarantee Your Lease. Many landlords are reluctant to rent their space to new businesses because they cannot be assured that the business will prosper. But the SBA can guarantee your loan for as much as $10,000 or more each month. Some small businesses have received a total guarantee of as much as $6 million. This, in turn, encourages landlords to rent to more small businesses.

Rebuilding Funds. If you are an unfortunate businessperson who has been singled out by some government agency because your product or service does not meet regulatory standards, you are not necessarily up the creek. The Small Business Administration can provide loans to certain businesses so that they can conform their product or services to the appropriate standards.

Expert Advice. In an effort to stimulate and promote small business throughout the country, the SBA has formed and supported a unique system of business guidelines under which experienced volunteers provide advice and counseling to any small-business person in need of assistance.

For more information about the SBA and the Small Business Investment Companies, contact your local office or the headquarters in Washington, D.C.

---

7 FRINGE BENEFITS IF YOU FORM YOUR OWN CORPORATION

Corporations get tax-free or tax-favored benefits that sole proprietors and partners do not. Here are 7 fringe benefits you can take advantage of if your business is incorporated:

1. *A Medical Reimbursement Plan.* A corporation that directly pays employees medical expenses can deduct these costs.

2. *Group Health Insurance.* A corporation can deduct the cost of the plan.

3. *Employee Death Benefits.* The first $5000 is tax free.

4. *Profit Sharing/Pension.* A corporation can contribute, tax free, up to 15 percent of an employee's salary to a pension or profit-sharing plan.

5. *Life Insurance Plans.* A corporation can deduct the cost of premiums for group life insurance.

6. *Deferred Salaries.* A corporate executive can defer a portion of his or her salary until retirement. At that time, he or she will be in a lower tax bracket and can receive the deferred part of the salary.

7. *Entertainment and Travel.* There is often a fine line between business and personal entertainment, and business-entertainment deductions are frequently hard for a private owner to prove. Since

corporations are rarely owned by one person, it is easier for them to convince the IRS that the deductions are applicable.

CAN YOU MAKE MONEY FRANCHISING?

You see them every day: fast food restaurants, convenience stores, automotive repair shops—all with big, nationally known names. What you may not realize, however, is that many of these establishments are run by local people under franchises. Is it for you?

What Is a Franchise? A franchise gives you the right to sell a company's product which is advertised and promoted on the national level. Depending on the product or company involved, the fee can be extremely high.

Are They Successful? A franchise is only as successful as the parent company. If it goes under, you will too, despite success at the local level. Nonetheless, it pays (and will cost you) to hook up with an established organization, for government statistics indicate that the failure rate of franchises is much smaller than that of individual, nonfranchised operations.

How Much Capital Do I Need? The amount needed to establish a franchise includes the initial investment, of course, plus enough money to keep you afloat for six months to a year. You may be talking about six figures.

How Do I Investigate? Information on franchises is found in business publications like *The Wall Street Journal* or *Forbes,* in newsletters published by industry trade associations, and in annual reports by the franchiser itself, including a profit and loss statement. Talk with franchisers about their profits and about problems such as labor, equipment maintenance, and utility costs. Do not deal with any franchiser who will not give you the names of its franchisees, and make sure you understand the terms of the agreement before you sign anything.

Here are 10 of the many questions you should get answers to before franchising:

1. How long has the company been in business and what is its record?
2. What is the quality of the product, and how well does it sell?
3. Is the territory exclusive and large enough for further expansion?
4. What is the competition like?
5. Can the contract be renewed, terminated, or transferred?
6. Under what conditions could the contract be terminated?
7. Do you pay a percentage to the parent?
8. Who is the supplier, how does he operate?
9. Are there standards for hiring, training, store layout, and inventory control?
10. Does the franchiser provide constant guidance if necessary?

There are many more things you need to know before it is safe to consider a franchise venture. And make sure you have confidence in the product and your ability to sell it. Otherwise you could wind up with a very expensive white elephant.

---

10 QUESTIONS TO ASK YOUR BUSINESS ACCOUNTANT

Your outside accountant can be one of the most valuable parts of your business. He or she has all of the records, and should be able to offer you sound advice—if you ask. Here are 10 questions you should always ask your accountant:

1. Will we need to borrow money during the coming year? If so, when?

2. Are all payroll deposits, tax returns, and estimated business-tax deposits up to date?

3. How can we reduce our accounts receivables?

4. Should we start fringe benefit plans which might result in a tax break?

5. The federal government requires holding on to certain records. Are they available?

6. Could we reduce our tax bill by forming a corporation, a subcorporation, or a partnership?

7. For corporations, have the necessary state annual reports been filed?

8. Are current billing, collecting, payroll, and other accounting procedures up to date? How could they be improved to save time and reduce mistakes?

9. Are certified financial statements a necessity?

10. Are there any noticeable losses due to poor internal security?

An outside accountant can do more than work on your books. He can probably be an important part of your business if you give him the chance.

WHAT TO DO WHEN YOU'RE IN THE RED

If you have large debts and don't think you can get your head above water, there are places you can go for help.

Counseling Services. Debt-reduction or credit counseling services are available in most cities. Each one is different; some will offer only advice, while others will see to it that your debt consolidation is handled properly. Some will even go as far as to pay your bills for you—with your money of course.

Beware of Deceptive Practices. Some counseling services do not tell their clients that there is no quick solution to their problem; that getting out from under could take years. Many people have been stuck with late payment or interest charges because the service didn't pay their bill in time. Check with the Better Business Bureau or local Consumer Affairs Department for information about debt-consolidation services.

17. COLLECTIBLES

"I bought this stamp for $20 four years ago. It's now worth $250."

Have you heard a statement like this lately? More and more people are getting into collectibles such as stamps, works of art, antiques, baseball cards, and precious gems. The list of collectibles is enormous. How about a bottle of 19th century Lafite-Rothschild? Or an autograph of a famous statesman or entertainer?

If you're interested in entering the collectibles market, you're probably wondering which ones are right for you. Which ones will appreciate in value? How does one go about purchasing rare stamps or coins? These questions and more will be answered in the following pages.

WHERE IS THE ANTIQUES MARKET?

If you have furniture and other items from before World War II, you just may be an important part of the next wave in antiques.

Antique dealers and auctioneers on both sides of the Atlantic think that the 1930s will provide a treasure chest of furniture, silver, and works of art.

British antique dealers expect items from the Edwardian age to increase in popularity—so much so, in fact, that Edwardian antiques may soon be worth double what they were just a few years ago. If you are moaning about all of the furniture from the 1930s that went to secondhand stores, don't fret. Experts predict there will soon be enough Depression-era antiques for you to make up what you got rid of.

PRINTS

With investors always looking for new markets to tap, limited editions of fine art have become very popular. You see the ads, in magazines or on television, for prints, medallions, or similar items. Will they appreciate in value? Here are 3 guidelines:

1. *How Limited Are Limited Editions?* If you deal with a reputable concern, then the print should indeed have a limited run. The original artist, who has a role in this decision, signs each print and marks the number of each on it. (2/100, for example, means you have the second copy of a 100-print run.)

2. *What Is a Print?* Do not confuse limited edition prints with reproductions. An original print, dealers say, is indeed a work of art, created specifically by the artist for that type of sale.

3. *How Is the Investment Value Determined?* As with any other collectible, demand will have the greatest impact on price. With art, however, there are a number of factors which cannot be measured that affect the value. Aesthetics are important, and so is the reputation of the artist. Original prints by respected artists like Chagall and Dali rise at staggering annual rates, 30 percent or more.

The quality of the print (the way it was made, not the art) is also very important, and it will be necessary for you to learn about different styles of art and printmaking in order to increase the chances that your prints will appreciate in value. You should be willing to hold on to your fine art for a considerable length of time, so make sure you like the work before buying it. The reason for this is quite simple: most of us can only afford to buy work by newer, less established artists. If and when these artists develop a following, your investment will then probably appreciate in value. In the meantime you will have to live with it.

4. *What Is Probably the Most Important Print Market in America Today?* The prices people are willing to pay for American art is skyrocketing. A quarter of a century ago, a print by Larry Rivers sold for a mere $75. Then they shot up to the $3500 range. Today they can go for as much as five times that amount.

But if you don't have a million dollars to invest, don't worry. You probably couldn't find a Remington for sale—or a Russell or a Bierstadt for that matter—even if you had the money. That is why the works of more contemporary Western artists are in such demand—and why their works are often snatched away before the oil has dried.

It is estimated that cowboy art is appreciating at the rate of 25 percent a year. How can you join this gold rush while the investing is still good? Let's begin by examining some of the major outlets for this genre.

Cowboys and Indians: An Investment Game in Which Everyone Wins. Put on your ten-gallon hat, hand-tooled boots and suede chaps, and prepare to enter the world of the wide-open range, where everyone packs a Colt .45 and chews tobacco. But don't worry. You won't have to rope cattle, get calloused hands, eat dust, or sleep in a bedroll. All you need to do is bring your checkbook. You are now ready for cowboy art.

The romance of the Western range was once the exclusive

domain of Hollywood and TV, but today it is the subject of one of the most exciting, explosive movements to capture the hearts and bankrolls of art investors.

What created this 1980s version of the gold rush, in which the treasure is not metal but canvas? It's simple—

Galleries. Western art is already an accepted genre, and many prestigious galleries handle the work of Western artists. Two of them are the Cowboy Hall of Fame, in Oklahoma City, Oklahoma, and the Petersen Galleries, in Beverly Hills, California.

Cowboy Artists of America. Cowboy Artists of America is the main outlet for the best in contemporary Western art. It is an association of Western artists that maintains the highest standards for admission. Cowboy Artists of America has its headquarters in Phoenix, Arizona, and conducts an annual sale and exhibition there every October. If you decide to go, you'd be well advised to get there early. Frequently, there is standing room only and the bidding is keen.

Independent Artists. There are also many fine artists who sell their works directly. These works are usually more reasonably priced. However, you're likely to find a greater variety of talent this way—and, consequently, a greater likelihood of investment error. Unless you know the market well, you may want to seek professional advice before buying from an independent artist.

For those who appreciate the value of its art, it's time to go West. The prices are still generally low and the potential for a good investment is there.

STAMP COLLECTING

As stamp collecting grows in popularity, good stamps become more and more valuable. How can you profit from stamps? What is the investment potential and what are the pitfalls? Here are 5 tips to consider:

1. *Find Out the Going Rate.* There is no reason to pay a higher price than the market value of a particular stamp unless you are lazy, careless, or both. *Linn's Stamp News* is the Bible when it comes to stamp collecting. Many dealers advertise their prices in this weekly publication, and it's a good way to measure previous or future purchases. Most stamp dealers carry it, but if you're unable to find it, you can write to PO Box 29, Sidney, Ohio 45365.

2. *Take Time to Find the Right Dealer.* Your local Yellow Pages will list every dealer in your area. Call each, and don't be afraid to ask for price quotes for particular stamps over the phone. When you get the lowest price for the stamp you're looking for, it's time to take a look at it.

3. *The Condition of the Stamp Is Crucial.* A rare stamp in terrible condition loses its value, so if you've paid a lot for it you've probably wasted your money. Insist on the following: The stamp should be in "very fine," never hinged, condition. Very fine means just that: no tears, stains, wrinkles, creases, short perforations, or hinge marks. The margins should be even on all four sides. The stamp should not be regummed—that only serves to cover up any hinge marks which were there prior to your purchase. Your untrained eye might not spot it, but someone you try to resell it to probably will.

4. *Certify the Condition.* Most reputable dealers will be glad to certify the condition of the stamp on your invoice. The information should include the exact condition of the stamp, along with a thirty-day, moneyback guarantee. If the stamp isn't everything the dealer said it was, you shouldn't have any trouble getting a full refund.

4. *Second Opinions.* Do not be embarrassed about showing the stamp to another dealer. He or she can assess the other

dealer's evaluation of that stamp and tell you if you made a wise purchase. Again, if the stamp isn't what it's cracked up to be, you can get a refund. Also, in checking with another dealer, that dealer may have a client interested in the stamp—which could mean a nice profit for you without much work. If you would prefer not to work with another dealer, a friend who collects stamps can probably evaluate the condition for you.

If you remember these tips, you should have no problem collecting stamps. You will assure yourself of getting the highest possible price when you decide to resell, and will find future purchases easy and hassle free.

INVESTING IN STAMPS

If you invest in stamps rather than collecting them for a hobby, you may want to have your portfolio managed.

What Is a Portfolio Manager? The person who manages your stamp collection can probably do for you what a stockbroker does for his or her clients: advise you on issues to purchase for investment value. You can save time by not having to go out and price stamps yourself; you have the advantage, if the firm is good, of having a network of stamp experts all over the world creating opportunities for you; and, if the portfolio management firm has collector clients, you will be able to sell your issues at the best possible price.

How Should I Pick a Portfolio Manager? Go by the firm's reputation. One that has a record of offering sound advice can make your investment pay off. A company that has offices around the world can find the best sales outlets. Bear in mind that a firm which will *buy* stamps back from you to sell to other collectors has your best interests in mind. This is very important, since many firms will only *trade* your stamps for those of other clients. A trade will not reflect true value as well as a sale. Take note of how long the firm says you should hold on to your stamps. Anyone who says that you can make a fast killing is probably misleading you. Expect to keep each issue at least five years before selling it. Most important, be sure you trust anyone who will have anything to do with managing your stamp portfolio. The less time you have to spend second-guessing the firm, the better.

INVESTING IN RARE WINES FOR PROFIT

If you are like most people, when you buy a bottle of wine, you buy it for dinner that evening and drink it. Some people, however, purchase a bottle of wine and enjoy it fifteen years later. Fewer still never drink it at all. These people are investors in rare vintage wines for profit, and their numbers are increasing.

A Valuable Investment. With interest in old wines soaring, there is every reason to believe that a bottle of vintage wine purchased now could be worth two or three times as much in three to five years. Beaulieu Vineyards' 1968 Cabernet Sauvignon from the winemaker's private reserve sold for $85 a case in 1972. In a recent auction, that case went for $1000. A case of 1981 Château Lafite-Rothschild that sold for $482 in 1973 went for $2583 at Christie's International Chicago auction in 1983.

Like stocks on the exchanges, wine prices rise and fall. There are people who will make a bundle on wine "futures" and others who will get burned. Unlike stocks, however, you can, in one lovely evening, drink up the potential profits.

There is another distinct difference between wine and stocks, besides the taste and drinkability. You can almost always find someone who wants to buy or sell a stock; millions of shares are traded every day. But trying to find a bottle of 1964 Lafite-Rothschild ten years from now could be like looking for a needle in a haystack. Most wine is not ready to drink when it arrives at your corner liquor store. But most liquor-store owners can't stay in business by keeping wine on their shelves for more than a decade, so they try to push it out as quickly as possible. What that means to you is that when a good wine is finally ready to drink, you probably won't be able to find it anymore. The solution to this problem? Buy early and buy often.

Buyers of large quantities of vintage wines are becoming as sophisticated as commodity futures traders. Before they buy, they want to know the answers to questions such as how much acreage a particular vineyard has or what kind of labor troubles they might expect—items that are more related to supply than to quality. Wine buying is turning into high-level economics. Here are 9 current hot wines that are difficult to get:

Burgundies

Richebourg 1959
La Tâche 1959
Romanée-Conti 1959
Musigny Comte de Vogüé 1959

The interesting thing about these wines is that they come from very small vineyards. These wines, which were relatively inexpensive when first bottled, have dramatically risen in price due to fears they will not be available.

White Wines

Montrachet 1964, 1971
Trockenbeerenauslese 1949

White wines have a shorter life span than red wines, which means they are generally unavailable by the time the red wines are ready to drink. Montrachets, "hyphenated" Montrachets, and German Beerenauslesen are still relatively inexpensive.

Blue-Chippers

The following wines are top priorities among wine investors. They are not yet ready to drink, but by the time they are, you may have trouble finding a bottle.

Margaux 1961
Haut-Brion 1961
Lafite-Rothschild 1961
Latour 1961

Prices of Some Vintage Wines. In the past few years, bottles of Lafite, from 1806 and 1822, have garnered $28,000 and $31,000, respectively. Several years ago, a New York sale saw $2900 paid for an 1878 Château Mouton-Rothschild. There were three bottles of this fine wine, and all were sold. At the same auction, one investor plunked down $2375 for a bottle of Château d'Yquem 1858.

A bottle of wine need not be over 100 years old to be considered good. The years 1959, 1966, and 1970 were all popular, and some of these vintages have disappeared from retailers' shelves. Stores that specialize in rare wines may have the vintage you are looking for in stock.

Most buyers of rare wine, say the experts, do not buy wines as an investment—leaving the field more open for you. There are 3 kinds of buyers:

1. People who buy a vintage for sentimental reasons: for example, the year they opened their business or in which a child was born.

2. Wine cellar owners who buy principally to fill out their own collection.

3. Those who invest in a rare bottle of wine in hopes that it will bring a handsome profit in a short period of time.

How to Get Into Rare Wines for Profit. What's true for other hobbies is true for rare wines. Study the commodity. There are many books on the market by so-called wine experts that rate particular vintages. Dealers that specialize in rare wine, like Sherry-Lehmann, 679 Madison Ave., New York, provide price lists and catalogues for their customers. You may be surprised to find you can get a vintage bottle for less than $400.

MOVIE POSTERS

Movie posters are big and getting bigger. What were once merely colorful pieces of paper are now avidly sought after. Rare Austrian and German movie posters, for example, were selling for as much as $6500 at a gallery exhibition in New York.

History. Between 1937 and 1961, over 200 million posters were printed to advertise American films. Produced en masse by a variety of art departments in major and independent movie studios, these posters were not considered to be of much value at the time. The craze for film posters started during the sixties, as demand for film memorabilia increased dramatically. People bought posters for small sums. Now, however, they are being displayed in museums and galleries and command very large amounts, sometimes as much as seventy times their original purchase price. For example, an original *Gone With the Wind* poster that cost $8 in 1968 is now worth over $500, a *Tol'able David* poster (1921) is worth about $400, and a large poster of *Citizen Kane* goes for $1000. All evidence points to even higher prices for rare movie posters in the future. A California collector paid $6000 a couple of years ago for an original six-sheet poster of the Lon Chaney version of *The Phantom of the Opera.*

Where to Find Posters. With the increasing interest in posters, there are a number of shops and antique stores which handle them. But they can be found virtually anywhere. One delighted collector found several hundred being used as insulation in a friend's home. Many people have found movie memorabilia in casual perusals of their attics and basements. Neighborhood garage sales are a good source.

Most posters of old films can be bought for $10 or less, and even the rarer ones found in galleries and antique shops usually run no more than a few hundred dollars.

You should know that foreign posters are considered more valuable than domestic ones, because they were usually made in smaller quantities and are usually of higher artistic quality. They are among the favorites of avid collectors.

The Value of Posters. As with most collectibles, the factor that most affects the price of a particular poster is its rarity. Because of television and radio advertising, the use of posters to advertise films is becoming less common than in the past. As posters in general become more and more scarce, this is a market whose value is going to increase.

Some commercial posters, such as the poster of Dino De Laurentiis' *King Kong,* were designed to be mass distributed and were produced in such large volume that they will probably not increase in value in the near future. But you never know when a sudden craze can up the prices. A long-ignored pastime, movie poster collecting is not only profitable, but can be an enjoyable reminder of your favorite films of the past.

TOY COLLECTING

It is no longer possible to think of toys as mere playthings, for these often-creative items for children have become collectibles for adults. Those train sets and old china dolls you once thought were merely taking up space and perhaps threw away are now among the most valuable toys around.

Not too long ago, $21,000 was paid for the 1905 Marklin model of the Weissenberg battleship, and someone doled out $18,000 for a cast-iron bank depicting Jonah and the Whale. In 1980, Sotheby Parke Bernet sold a train set for $8500. These are only a few examples of the high value of toys. Generally, as with most collectibles, the older and rarer the item, the higher the value. But valuable collectibles can often be only ten years old, and many contemporary collections contain relatively new toys no longer on the market.

Doll Collecting. For years, collecting dolls, marionettes, and doll furniture has been popular. Dolls, with their fixed expressions and intricate garb, have mesmerized both children and adults for centuries. They are also one of the easiest things to collect. One woman in Washington has an international collection of dolls so large that she hardly has room to store them all.

Types of Doll Collections. Many collectors decide to concentrate on one type of doll. This can make it easier to track down missing elements in your collection. For example, you could specialize in brocaded dolls from the Renaissance, china dolls from the 17th century, or wax dolls from the Elizabethan era. Some people also decide to collect dolls made from a particular material—such as plastic, wood, or papier-mâché—or dolls from a particular region or historical era. Dolls from Africa and Asia, for instance, are often sought after for their elaborate costumes made from beads, silver, gold, and colored cloth. The most expensive doll collection is one consisting of 17th- and 18th-century dolls. Miniature dolls are another costly collector's item.

But it's not only expensive dolls that collectors go after. So-called "poor" dolls—ones made of rags, paper, or celluloid—have become popular over the years. Wooden dolls from countries such as Haiti are also inexpensive and can form an impressive collection.

Doll Furniture. Investing in doll furniture can run into money for the serious collector. The most valuable pieces are those from earlier eras, because they generally are the best crafted and serve as records of their epoch.

The tradition of including miniature furniture when selling dolls began in the Netherlands, where they exported dolls with trousseaus, bedroom furniture, and household items. Often, these miniature pieces were reproduced down to the last detail. Many of these items are still available at antique dealers for reasonable prices.

Model Trains. Model train collecting has become a popular pastime throughout America and abroad. Many train fanatics began their hobby either by receiving a train set as a child or by giving one to a child. However they initially received a model train, once collectors become hooked there's no stopping them. A shopowner in Tokyo has developed a miniature railroad system of over seventy square yards. Most collectors, however, have smaller-scale collections, such as miniature models.

The first model trains, manufactured in the 1860s, were powered by steam and utilized doughnut-shaped rails stamped out of sheet metal. Following that came the development of clockwork locomotives, which were soon followed by electric trains. The earliest electric trains operated on A.C. power conducted through only one rail. They could not run in reverse until about twenty years ago, when D.C. power made reversal possible. This eliminated the need for a center rail and made the trains more practical.

AIRCRAFT MODELS

While model airplanes have captivated collectors for years, only recently have they become popular as collectors' items—both as an investment and as a hobby. The unique thing about aircraft models is that collectors must literally put together their investment, for the personal touch is highly regarded by the serious collector. Pre-made models are frowned upon and are therefore less valuable. Connoisseurs also demand that the models be as close as technically possible to the original. This applies to models of warships and cars as well.

The International Plastic Modeller's Society (IPMS), in London, has set the general standard for the scale and size of models. They also consider the authenticity of a model, establishing how true to the original it is.

Because assembling these models involves a great deal of work and time, it is not surprising that there are few large collections. In addition, these items are among the most delicate and fragile of collectibles. Nonetheless, they continue to fascinate and excite the collector interested in detail, style, and craftsmanship.

GOOD NEWS FOR BASEBALL CARD COLLECTORS

A new wrinkle has been added to baseball card collecting as a result of a court ruling late last year. The decision challenged the exclusive right of Topps Chewing Gum to manufacture major league baseball cards and has opened the door for two new entries in the field, Fleer (Philadelphia) and Donruss (Memphis) issued major league baseball cards for the first time in 1981. Some mail order houses have priced each set at less than $16 for 660 Fleer cards (500 full color) and 528 Donruss cards in mint, boxed, and unopened condition. The 1981 Topps set is priced slightly higher for more than 700 cards.

If you've never collected before, here are 3 things to remember:

1. Individual cards, with rare exceptions, are not worth much. What are valuable are complete player sets. For example, a Willie Mays card for every year he appeared—probably more than twenty-five cards, if you include those in which he appeared as "Home Run Champ" or "Most Valuable Player."

2. As with stamps, mint condition is the difference between being valuable and extremely valuable. That being the case, keep your cards in inexpensive plastic sheets for display.

3. There are two publications that will give you an idea of what cards are wanted and the going price. *The Baseball Advertiser,* with a circulation of more than 70,000, is published six times each year. The *Sport American Baseball Card Price and Guide* has a list and values of almost every card in existence.

Baseball card collecting has become a bonanza in recent years. There are always sales, auctions, and displays to go to for the novice or the serious collector.

PHOTOGRAPHY

Photograph collecting is fast becoming a booming business. A main appeal of this enterprise is that you need not spend more than a few hundred dollars to own a print by an important photographer. For example, a print by Bill Brandt is about $300; a Lewis Hine, $150 to $225. A large Richard Avedon is $750. A Stieglitz recently sold for $4500. Almost every vintage print has gone up ten times or more. A 19th-century print by Julia Margaret Cameron sold for $20 in 1963. Today, the same print is worth up to $2000.

Another way that photographs gain in value is when an important photographer dies. Diane Arbus's portrait prints sold for $150 before her death in 1971. Now they fetch $1000 or more.

Here are 6 rules to follow, in order of their importance, in determining the value of a print:

1. The most valuable prints are those that were developed and signed by a noted photographer at the time the negative was made.
2. Next in importance are ones printed and signed later by the photographer.
3. Following that are prints made by the photographer, but which he or she didn't sign.
4. Next, prints made by someone else and signed by the photographer.
5. After that are unsigned prints made after the photographer's death by a noted craftsman.
6. Last in importance are prints made by an unknown regardless of who took the original picture.

A growing concern among collectors is the whereabouts of the original negative, since an unlimited number of prints can be made from them. Experts say that the photographer doesn't want to lessen the value of his or her prints by overprinting them, which should ease collectors' concerns. Also, the artist would rather be shooting new subjects than spending long hours in the darkroom making prints. Still, there is no guarantee that more prints cannot be made. One suggestion in buying photographs is to look for numbered prints. Photographers can be sued if they make more prints than they originally warranted they would.

As in any rapidly growing industry, the standards change. One thing is certain: the hobby of collecting old photographs seems destined to expand in the years to come.

MAPS: A NEW AVENUE FOR COLLECTORS

Old maps are becoming as collectible as old stamps, rare books, or vintage wine.

A Hobby That's Just Beginning to Take Off. The number of map collectors has doubled in the past ten years, but it's still a gray area as far as investment value is concerned. The main problem is that it's an unknown quantity; nobody has a firm handle on exactly what is rare and what is abundant. As an investment opportunity, it's strictly long term.

Why Collect Maps? Maps have evolved with world history. As empires have crumbled and new nations appeared, maps have recorded these transformations on paper or other material. People collect maps because of the stories they tell and because maps often reflect the aesthetic canons and world view of their period. Their art work, lettering, and design comment on their epoch the way paintings do.

What to Collect. It is best to concentrate on a period in history or a part of the world you are interested in—a country where you have lived or worked, a region your ancestors settled in. Maps from the 20th century are not going to appreciate for a long time, so most collectors look for ones made at least before the turn of the century.

Some Examples of Long-Term Appreciation. A map of America, made in the 16th century, is worth almost $5000. It sold in 1961 for less than $150. A 1775 map depicting the Great Lakes region brought $35 dollars twenty years ago. It is now worth $750. As you can see, this is definitely a long-term investment. How long you are willing to wait, of course, depends on you.

3 Tips for Potential Investors:

1. Read some reference books and bone up on cartography before you buy anything.

2. Look at as many originals as possible. Reproductions will not give you the same feel for maps as originals will.

3. Discuss your objectives with a dealer and look at his or her selection. Follow your interests and you won't be talked into buying anything you don't want.

A Final Note. Map collecting is still unknown to most investors. Interest may soar, but it will take some time. Remember that stamp collecting was in its infancy just a few decades ago, and there are now 16 million philatelists.

18. PRECIOUS METALS, GEMS, AND COINS

They are as popular as they are valuable—gold, silver, platinum, and other metals that are continuing to hold the interest of investors. Here is important information on what you should know about them.

---

8 THINGS TO KNOW BEFORE YOU BUY PRECIOUS GEMS

With inflation temporarily down but threatening to rise again at any time, investors continue to buy precious gems as a hedge against economic instability. Remember:

1. You don't have to be rich to buy precious gems. Although diamond prices have, in general, increased over the past decade, rubies, sapphires, and emeralds can still be found at reasonable prices.

2. Gems are almost certain to appreciate, if not immediately then over the years. The cost of living has more than doubled over the past twenty years, and there is no sign that the end is in sight. The trend is for continuing investment in this medium,

which should push prices higher. But don't plan on selling your gems for a profit right away.

3. Make sure you know whom you are buying from. Most experts agree that you should purchase gems only from reputable, established dealers. Explain to the dealer what you want and how much you're willing to spend. Look at a variety of stones before making a purchase.

4. There is some room to negotiate. The retail markup on precious gems runs anywhere from 30 to 50 percent, so you can probably get a better deal if you buy larger gems. Even those dealers with big reputations and prices to match will usually negotiate for investment-quality stones.

5. Get a second opinion. An outside appraisal from either another jeweler or an independent appraiser is a necessity. A check of local jewelers will help you find one.

6. Have the gem certified. The Gemological Institute of America will do this for a reasonable fee. The GIA has offices at 1180 Avenue of the Americas, New York, NY, and 1660 Stewart St., Santa Monica, CA, and accepts mail inquiries if sent registered. If the jeweler has already had the stone certified, there is no reason for you to duplicate the process.

7. There are specific aesthetic guidelines that will affect the future value of precious gems. For diamonds, the whiter the color and the fewer the flaws, the greater the value. With colored stones, the depth of color and the degree of clarity are the biggest factors.

8. Insure your gems. This is an additional expense, but a necessary one. The cost is different in each state and for each insurer. If you keep them in a safe deposit box, vault insurance is available.

Auctions and museum showings are a good way to educate yourself in this field. There are also a number of books on the market which serve as good guidelines to gem collecting.

DIAMONDS

You've heard the rumblings before. Stern warnings about the dangers of diamond investing. Maybe you've ignored them, maybe you haven't. Here's a closer look:

Price Increases. Any price hike at the wholesale level of diamonds will almost certainly be felt by the consumer. The reason for this is the control of the industry by the De Beers organization, which owns about 85 percent of the world's supply of rough stones. So any price hike by them is felt virtually across the board.

High-Grade Stones Are in Short Supply. A diamond cutter ("sight buyer") is considered lucky if a sealed purchase consists of 25 to 30 percent investment-quality stones. The rest are of a lesser quality, and many dealers are being pressured into unloading these stones first.

There Are Unscrupulous Dealers. A London price increase is a ticket to ride for many telephone and mail-order bucket shops. Any time there is a price hike, they crank up their operations and thousands of investors are defrauded. Common tricks involve the substitution of zircons for diamonds, switching the stone you want for one of a poorer quality, and switching gem lab certificates. Keep your eye out for dealers who certify their own stones. Purchase only diamonds certified by the Gemological Institute of America or the European Gemological Laboratory.

Other Forms of Protection. Besides the independent certification of a stone, a laser photograph or a foil impression of the stone can be taken. Each is unique. Some companies sell insurance to protect you if you don't get the stone you ordered.

Everybody's Got a Piece of the Action. Financial advisers, attorneys, and insurance representatives who sell diamonds to investors get commissions of 2 to 5 percent. Get the name of the supplier and check his or her credentials. *Do not* get involved in any deal that requires cash up front for someone to make a purchase for you.

Some Companies Are Working to End Dishonesty. A small group of diamond merchants has banded together to form the Diamond Dealers Club in an effort to police the industry without government interference. Their address is 30 W. 47th St., New York, NY 10019.

INVESTING IN SEMIPRECIOUS STONES

As investors look for new ways to place their money, the interest in semiprecious gems has increased. Here is a look at some of the reasons for this, and 10 tips:

1. *Why the Interest?* Many investors have been priced out of the very lucrative precious stones market. High-quality diamonds are selling for more than $20,000 a carat, rubies for $10,000 a carat. By comparison, some second-tier stones sell for as little as $100 a carat. Even the most sought after stones, like tourmalines, garnets, spinels, and topazes rarely go for more than $1000 a carat.

2. *A Potential Market Exists.* Every investment has its own risks, but experts say the increase in investor interest could push prices up by as much as 50 to 100 percent. The aquamarine, for example, has doubled in value in less than two years, to $650 a carat.

3. *Best Bets.* Blood-red tourmalines are now $325 a carat; blue-green tourmalines, $250; rubellite, a reddish variety, $200. The price range for garnets is much wider: from $100 to $1100.

4. *A Coattail Effect.* Some of these gems have experienced a rise in demand because of their similarity to other precious stones. Ruby spinel has more than doubled in value lately to $1800 a

carat, largely because it looks like a ruby. The ruby is advancing 10 percent a month in its own right, and some observers feel the spinel will be right behind.

5. *Choosing a Dealer.* Because of the increased demand, many diamond dealers are jumping on to the colored stones bandwagon without a great deal of knowledge. A small color difference can have a startling effect on the price. There are also many synthetic or doctored stones around. Only an expert can spot a fake stone. To avoid risk, choose a dealer who has sold semiprecious stones for more than three years. Ask him or her for credentials, and insist upon references. You might even consider asking for a recent financial statement.

6. *What About Price?* You can expect a markup of 25 to 33 percent from most dealers, although some will charge more. Buy a stone of at least one carat, of the best quality you can get.

7. *Determining Quality.* As mentioned before, the color of a stone can drastically affect its price. The cut and flawlessness of a semiprecious stone are not as important as those of a diamond, but both will be factors in determining the price and resale value.

8. *Selling Your Semiprecious Stones.* You can expect the resale of semiprecious stones to be an arduous process. Unlike diamonds, there are no uniform rating standards for them, and appraisals are highly subjective. Finding a buyer at the right price could take months.

9. *Hold On, Help Is Coming.* The Gemological Institute of America, the trade group that initiated diamond grading, is devising a system for measuring and recording gem color. These procedures could be the first step toward a universally accepted method of grading semiprecious stones.

10. *The Potential Remains.* For the present, there are a number of risks involved in the purchase of semiprecious stones. The best advice right now is not to invest in stones unless you have the patience to hold on to them for at least two to five years.

In the 1970s, gold experts scoffed at the possibility of gold rising to over $800 an ounce, which is what happened in late 1979. And in spite of the decline in the gold price, many investment counselors say the yellow metal is still a smart buy to head off inflationary pressures that will reappear in the next few years. The boldest speculators predict $1000 or more an ounce, in spite of the fact that they were wrong about this in 1980.

In any case, just as people with foresight buy fire and theft insurance to protect their possessions, they are learning to stock gold in case of *financial* emergency. Even those who are uninformed about the complexities of the gold market are making small investments in bullion coins such as the Krugerrand and the Canadian Gold Leaf.

The Small Investor. Unfortunately, it is almost always the big-time investors who reap the real profits in gold. Only they can buy, for example, large bars or bricks, which is the cheapest way to purchase gold and provides the greatest profits. But there is no reason why the modest investor can't get in on the action. Stashing a supply of 1-ounce coins could eventually be very profitable, given the uncertain economic climate.

Coins. As mentioned earlier, coins like the Krugerrand are among the most popular investments. Each of these coins weighs about 1 ounce. Be certain you're getting your money's worth, because it is easy for unscrupulous dealers to defraud you.

The main problem with investing in these coins, however, is the premium. You usually end up paying anywhere from 4 to 10 percent more than the value of the gold content because of the minting, marketing, and other costs. It is sometimes possible to strike a bargain with the dealer if you are purchasing in substantial quantities.

Selling Your Gold Jewelry. It is not a good idea to go rummaging through your jewelry chest to sell everything with the slightest gold content helter-skelter. Don't expect to make a killing right away. When you decide that there is jewelry you have no use for, take time out and consider your options. First of all, remember that jewelry is very seldom made of pure gold. A piece that says 14 karat gold on it probably contains only 58 percent gold. Jewelry made of 18 and 22 karat gold will undoubtedly command a higher price.

Dealers who buy your gold usually melt it down into bars and sell it to jewelers and for industrial purposes. That is why when you walk into the office of a precious metals dealer, they usually weigh the gold content of your pieces first. After they peck away at their calculators, they usually make you an offer. If they hem and haw, and try to bargain with you, it means they are probably not giving you as much as another dealer might.

Shop around. Other dealers might offer you more. At any rate, you get a better idea of what you can get for your merchandise.

Timing is also important. It helps to know the current gold quotes. You will find that they change in as little as half an hour. After lunch, your gold could be worth much less than what it was that morning.

Never sell your pieces strictly for their gold content if you believe there is significant craftsmanship or other valuable elements to it. One woman sold a gold-laced brooch for the amount the gold was worth, only later to find that the precious stone in the middle of it was worth three times as much as the gold.

What Is Gold? Only 24-karat gold is pure gold. Anything with a lesser label contains other metals. Items that are soldered, like necklaces, bracelets, and pins, can contain up to 1, more or less, karat of the gold content they are labeled with. The Department of Consumer Affairs in New York has found many 14-karat-labeled bracelets to be of lesser gold content.

Gold Fever Attracts Thieves and Counterfeiters. If you buy gold, you will of course want to keep it in a safe place. For centuries

Europeans have hidden their gold in their fields and backyards. Some Americans are also mistrustful of banks and bank vaults, and even fear government confiscation. So they store gold in their home safes, attics, or basements. This is generally unsafe and unwise. Bank deposit boxes are the best place for your precious metals.

Alternatives. Some investors have found that *gold certificates* are much more convenient than hauling bars of gold or sacks of coins around with them. These certificates can usually be purchased in $1000 denominations and can be sold in fractional denominations.

GOLD FEVER: THE PROFITS AND PITFALLS

Gold has been linked to some form of currency since Roman times. Under the gold standard established in modern times, it was possible for central banks to sell their gold for currency when currency was low and buy gold when currency was in surplus. This standard carried throughout the civilized world. The value of different currencies was thereby balanced out, and there was much less tendency for inflation in the world as a whole. Fluctuations in world price levels did occur, but for the most part shifts in the gold price were very moderate.

When the United States Federal Reserve Bank was created in 1913, the government began to engage in deficit financing on a large scale and hasn't stopped since. This clearly affected global prices. When World War II created a new credit inflation, followed by the Korean War dollar inflation, gold was scarce at $35 an ounce.

In the late 1950s gold became more undervalued and was used less in the balance of payment settlement. Consequently, effective monetary reserves were cut. Europe began to fear dollar devaluation in 1970 and asked for gold instead of dollars, which helped prompt President Nixon to suspend gold convertibility. Since then, monetary restraint, or lack thereof, has been decided by major bankers.

Gold mining stocks appear to still be in an uptrend despite reversals. Major mines are found in South Africa, Canada, the United States and Australia, and spectacular profits have been made by trading them. It is important that you read the recommendations of forecasters who specialize in this area before investing, for these stocks are extremely volatile. *Barron's* weekly carries advertisements for many worthwhile newsletters. *The Dines Letter,* PO Box 22, Belvedere, CA, contains excellent information on this subject.

In spite of setbacks, the gold rush is still going on, and probably will be for many years to come. Economic factors, such as the destabilization caused by unemployment, and political factors, such as Soviet and Iranian aggression, seem to ensure high gold prices.

STRATEGIC METALS

If unpredictable fluctuations in gold and silver prices have you baffled, it may be time to turn your attention to strategics. According to some experts, it will be the boom market of the late 1980s.

What's a Strategic? Strategics are rare metals vital in the production of steel, semiconductors, and military hardware. They include titanium, platinum, manganese, cobalt, and chromium.

Why Invest in Them? Experts say there are 2 reasons:

1. Much of the U.S. supply is imported from southern Africa and the Soviet Union. The political instability in Africa is an ongoing problem that could result in situations similar to what we've seen with oil in the Mideast.

2. President Reagan's determination to increase military spending has automatically created the ongoing need for these metals.

An Example of a Politically Motivated Price Rise. Several years ago, Angolan rebels crossed into the neighboring country of Zaire and took over a cobalt mine which was responsible for 65 percent of the free world's supply. The spot market price of cobalt increased from less than $7 to $45 a pound. Although the price eventually settled in at $25, the increase was enough to cause a dramatic rise in the cost of some weapons.

Aren't I Really Betting Against the U.S.? The experts say no: the price increases will occur regardless of speculative activity. They add that private stockpiling by investors will increase the supply available to the government and thus help protect the free world against political opportunism.

How Do I Invest? The most direct way is to order specific commodities through a broker. There are no exchanges for buying or selling strategics, so most negotiations are handled directly with metals dealers. You can also invest in companies that do most of their business in this field, usually producers of the particular metals.

Things You Should Know. Unlike buying a commodities future, you are obligated to take delivery of the materials, which means you must pay for storage and insurance. You will not collect any interest while the value of the metals appreciates. There is also the possibility of manipulation of world markets, and there are experts who suspect that may already be happening with some strategics.

MINT COINS AND MEDALLIONS

Manufacturers of gold coins and medallions like the Franklin Mint are on the defensive. Critics charge that their products are not the hedges against inflation that they have been advertised to be. Well, Franklin and its competitors have apparently been vindicated. Because of the 1981 rise in gold and silver prices, many people who bought coins and medals found themselves with a quick and easy profit. At the height of the gold and silver fever, some dealers were buying mint products at extremely high prices—sometimes more than 100 percent of what the mint originally charged. The mints, although happy they were temporarily off the hook, said that their products are designed as collectibles, that anyone looking for a fast buck should be investing in bullion, not medallions and coins. In fact, the collectibles market declined in 1983—just as rapidly as the metals market—proving both arguments to be false!

MAKING MONEY IN RARE COINS

If you are thinking about taking a chance on gold but are wary of fluctuations in the market, rare coins may be the answer.

A Hedged Bet. Rare gold coins, as opposed to bullion or restrikes, offer a twofold investment: the value of the gold itself and that of the coin as a collector's item. The latter offers some protection when gold prices dip.

Gold Coins May Go Up in Value Before Gold Does. The interest in rare gold coins is not a recent phenomenon. Even before the gold mania struck, the price of the coins reflected a general turn away from the inflated dollar. One analyst says rare coins rose in value 13 percent a year from 1968 to 1978, well ahead of the inflation rate of the time. In 1983, however, they declined almost as rapidly.

Their Value Will Increase. Professional speculators are thinking big when it comes to rare coins, and there's good reason for their collective optimism in the light of some recent astounding sales of gold coins. *Item:* November 1980. The famous Garrett coin collection, owned by Johns Hopkins University, in Baltimore, is auctioned off for an incredible $7 million. A single coin, the 1787 Brasher Doubloon, sold for an unprecedented $725,000. *Item:* In 1983, a large New York dealer put up for sale a set of 1906 $10 and $20 gold eagles. "Liberty-Large" proofs and uncirculated specimens make up the set. The price? $1 million for the set.

Deciding What to Collect. Gold coins have been around from the first hint of recorded history. The Greeks made coins which the Romans collected. The Romans manufactured coins which were in turn collected during the Renaissance. Larger banks in Switzerland and West Germany have departments whose sole job is to find rare European coins. In the U.S., few dealers specialize in foreign or ancient coins. The necessary expertise is too great, and the condition of the coins is not always the best.

What to Buy. Although you will probably be limited to U.S. issues, there is no reason why you cannot specialize your collection. There are 2 essential factors:

1. *Quality.* If you can get ten coins for the price of one, take the more expensive coin. The quality will be better, and the dealer's markup will probably be less.

2. *Top Grades Only.* The better the quality, the greater the chances of its increasing in value. Stick to the following: brilliant coins struck as proofs, regular coins that have never been circulated, and the least worn of circulated currency coins (listed as extra fine or very fine).

There Are No Guarantees. Like any other commodity, coin

values tend to be cyclical. During the recession of 1974 the value of rare gold coins dropped, only to rise again.

A Note About Silver Dollars. Silver dollars are worth buying and holding. During the silver boom tons of these once common coins were melted down for their silver, which of course reduced their supply radically and increased the worth of the ones that were left.

"Mint Sets" and Bullion Coins. Coin experts warn about the heavily advertised "mint sets" such as the one hyped by the Treasury Department for $6 over face value. If there is no silver in these, their worth will never increase by much. And "collectors' medallions" like the ones sold by the Franklin Mint will have no value whatsoever as rarities, even though some gold and silver is present. Contemporary bullion coins such as the South African Krugerrand, and restrikes such as the Mexican 50-peso piece, are not expected to have future value to collectors.

Don't Go in Blind. Professionals are unanimous on one point: know the product before you start to collect it. It will help you in decision making and protect you from being cheated. The basics of coin collecting are not that complex. They can be learned in a couple of months. *The Complete Book of Coin Collecting,* by Joseph Coffin (Coward, McCann & Geoghegan), is excellent for beginners. Available in paperback.

Things to Look Out For. Counterfeiting has been around as long as coins have, and any rare coin that looks too good to be true probably is. There are firms, however, that authenticate gold coins. Go to a reputable dealer or contact the American Numismatic Association, PO Box 2366, Colorado Springs, CO 80901.

A far more serious problem than counterfeiting is the alteration of dates and mint marks, which drastically changes the value of a coin. The 1901 silver dollar is a prime example. One that has been in circulation is worth about $20; one that has never been circulated, or just appears to be in mint condition, is worth about $500. You can see the problem.

Miscellaneous Notes. Figure on keeping your coins at least two years to allow them to appreciate. One other rule of thumb: *Do Not Touch.* Handling causes wear, which reduces value. A safety deposit box may be the best place for them, especially given the extremely high cost of insurance ($20 per $1000 of value). Another reason to keep coins in a deposit box is the tax laws: collectors are not eligible for certain tax deductions, such as the expense of going to coin sales and auctions, which investors can take. If you keep your coins in a bank, the IRS considers you an investor; if they are in your home, you are a collector. A sticky point, but it can save you some money.

19.
RETIREMENT

Will you be able to retire comfortably? Rising prices make it increasingly difficult. Will you be able to cope?

Whether you are retiring next month or ten years from now, learn how to protect your pension and how to get the most from Social Security—two important considerations for the prospective retiree who is concerned about making ends meet.

THE FUTURE OF PENSIONS

Millions of Americans rely on their pensions to help them survive after retirement. Inflation, however, can make private pensions worth less and less.

Less Purchasing Power. With the cost of living increasing by approximately 8 percent annually over the last decade, persons who retired in 1974 have found their pensions worth 50 percent less in terms of real dollars. Many companies offer some sort of cost-of-living increase, but it's hardly enough to keep pace with inflation. With 10 percent annual inflation, a fixed pension will lose two-thirds of its value in ten years.

An Older Society. Inflation poses a great threat, particularly since Americans are living longer. An average sixty-five-year-old can now expect to live until eighty, which means he or she will be drawing pension benefits for fifteen years. The number of elderly is increasing, and many of them combine their pensions with Social Security benefits in order to live. The Social Security System has been on the brink of collapse several times and unless pension benefits are adjusted for inflation, severe problems could arise for the nation's elderly if it does finally go under.

Inadequate Pensions May Have a Spillover Effect. If older Americans can't live on their pensions, we could see disastrous results throughout the economy:

1. *Social Security.* Benefits would have to be increased in the wake of worthless pensions. This would increase the tax burdens on working Americans, create higher inflation, and possibly make it impossible to balance the federal budget.

2. *Capital investment.* Because companies use pension fund money to invest, productivity would inevitably decline for lack of capital.

3. *Social Problems.* Working Americans would resent paying the freight of older people in the form of higher payroll taxes for Social Security, and would also be extremely unhappy about the declining value of their own future pensions. This could lead to even more tax cheating than exists now, and possibly to political destabilization.

What's Being Done. Many companies are offering periodic increases to pensioners as a way of helping them cope with inflation. There is also increasing pressure on Congress to increase the number of tax-free retirement savings plans and to specify cost-of-living increases for private pensions. Companies are urging their employees to plan for retirement by investing outside of their pension. Experts are also hopeful that the Age Discrimination in Employment Act will stem the tide of early retirements that have taken place in the past few years. All of these steps should go a long way toward helping the pensioner, but unless the inflation rate can be brought down even more, and kept down, it all may be for naught.

---

10 IMPORTANT FACTS ABOUT YOUR SOCIAL SECURITY

1. Nine out of every ten American workers, over 34 million men, women, and children, are covered under some form of Social Security.
2. As early as age sixty-two, you can begin to receive benefits. Survivors and dependents of workers can also receive them.
3. Your contributions, as a worker, to Social Security are part of the benefits you receive if you retire or become disabled, or which your family can receive if you die.
4. Benefits are adjusted to cost-of-living increases.
5. Before you or your family can qualify for benefits, you must have a certain amount of work credit on your side.
6. The amount of work credit required depends on your age at retirement, death, or when you become disabled.
7. The amount of your benefits will depend on your average earnings over a period of years.
8. In 1978, a new method of calculating benefits went into effect. Earnings are updated in consideration of gradual increases over the years.
9. You have to apply for Social Security benefits in order to determine what they are.
10. If you want to know more about Social Security benefits, you should contact your local Social Security Administration of-

fice. Ask for a copy of the brochure called *Estimating Your Social Security Retirement Check.*

10 WAYS TO GET THE MOST FROM SOCIAL SECURITY

If you are a typical office or factory worker, you have no doubt watched with dismay as your paycheck has been chipped away at for Social Security deductions. You may feel even more helpless when it comes time to receive your benefits and you are not sure how to go about it. Here are 10 ways you probably never knew about to get the most out of your Social Security:

1. It is now possible to receive a refund of up to $10,000 for Social Security payments that were wrongly taken from your paycheck, for you do not have to make Social Security payments for earnings beyond a certain amount (which changes each year).

Think about your situation. How much have you earned and how much have you paid out in Social Security? Find out the current limit of withholdings on earnings and determine if you have accidently overpaid. If you have had more than one job, the possibility of this happening is even greater.

Contact your nearest Social Security office and tell them you would like your account investigated. They'll send you the forms. Fill them out, return them, and you'll find out if you're entitled to a refund.

2. You can collect Social Security before you're sixty-five. It is possible to begin receiving benefits as early as sixty-two if you are no longer working. You do, however, receive reduced benefits.

3. The best way to get as much as you are entitled to in benefits is to inquire directly at your local Social Security office. They will give you detailed information about the system, list all

the possible benefits you may qualify for, and tell you exactly how much you are entitled to receive. Even before you near the retirement stage, it is a good idea to know exactly what you'll be getting later.

4. You can boost your payments as high as $1281 each month by claiming every single individual whom you support, including children, parents, and other relatives.

5. Returning to the work force does not always mean that you lose your benefits or have them reduced. A new job may place you in a higher bracket and thereby increase them.

6. It is possible for your wife to collect monthly Social Security checks, even if you are divorced. If you are a divorcée and depend on your ex-husband for support, it is possible for you to receive large monthly checks, particularly if you have children to support.

7. Parents can also collect on their children's accounts if the parents live with the children, depend on them for money, food, clothing, etc., and if they are unable to work. All the children have to do is claim their parents as dependents.

8. Children can collect as much as $301 a month from Social Security. Any dependent child under eighteen years of age who is unmarried can receive benefits if the parents are entitled.

9. Some recipients of Social Security can return to school and earn as much as they like and not lose any benefits. This is a boon for those at sixty-five who are not ready to throw in the sponge.

10. Some women are entitled to more than $700 a month in the event of the sudden death of their breadwinner spouse.

20. WHERE TO GO NEXT Sources of Free Information and Services

Where do you go when you want specific questions and answers about your home, finances, and investments? This book is the first step, but there are also hundreds of free publications you can send for. Many of these pamphlets, fact sheets, and brochures are published by U.S. government agencies: the Department of Housing and Urban Development, the Department of Health and Human Services, and the Energy Department among them. You can obtain a complete list at any time by contacting:

Superintendent of Documents
U.S. Government Printing Office
Washington, D.C. 20402
(202) 783-3238

In addition to the Government Printing Office in Washington, many major cities have U.S. Government bookstores. They can provide you with quicker service than Washington can. The following is a list of those bookstores and their addresses:

Atlanta Bookstore
Room 100
Federal Building
275 Peachtree St. ND
Atlanta, GA 30303

Birmingham Bookstore
Room 102A
2121 Eighth Ave. N.
Birmingham, AL 35203

Boston Bookstore
Room G25
John F. Kennedy Federal Building
Sudbury St.
Boston, MA 02203

Canton Bookstore
Federal Office Building
201 Cleveland Ave. SW
Canton, OH 44702

Chicago Bookstore
Room 1463
Everett McKinley Dirksen Building
219 S. Dearborn St.
Chicago, IL 60604

Dallas Bookstore
Room 1046
Federal Building—U.S. Courthouse
1100 Commerce St.
Dallas, TX 75202

Denver Bookstore
Room 1421
Federal Building, U.S. Courthouse
1961 Stout St.
Denver, CO 80202

Detroit Bookstore
Room 229
Federal Office Building
231 W. Lafayette Blvd.
Detroit, MI 48226

Kansas City Bookstore
Room 135
Federal Office Building
601 E. 12th St.
Kansas City, MO 64106

Los Angeles Bookstore
Room 1015
Federal Office Building
300 N. Los Angeles St.
Los Angeles, CA 90012

New York Bookstore
Room 110
26 Federal Plaza
New York, NY 10007

Philadelphia Bookstore
Main Lobby
U.S. Post Office

9th and Chestnut Streets
Philadelphia, PA 19107

Pueblo Bookstore
PDDC
PO Box 713
Pueblo, CO 81001

San Francisco Bookstore
Room 1023
Federal Office Building
450 Golden Gate Ave.
San Francisco, CA 94102

Nongovernmental and Governmental Groups

Many lobbies and public interest organizations publish pamphlets or newsletters with important information. When requesting material, include a stamped, self-addressed envelope. The following is a list of some of the best (there are thousands more):

Cooperative Housing—A Consumer Guide
National Association of Housing Cooperatives
1012 14th St. NW
Suite 805
Washington, D.C. 20006

Questions About Condominiums—What to Ask Before You Buy
(Publication HUD-77-H (6))
Dept. of Housing and Urban Development
Public Service Center
451 7th St.
Washington, D.C. 20410

Protecting Your Home Against Theft
(Publication HUD-315-F (5))
Dept. of Housing and Urban Development
Public Service Center
451 7th St.
Washington, D.C. 20410

Tips on Home Improvement
(Publication 02205)
Better Business Bureau
1150 17th St. NW
Washington, D.C. 20036

Home Buyer's Vocabulary
(Publication HUD-383-H (4))
Dept. of Housing and Urban Development
Public Service Center
451 7th St.
Washington, D.C. 20410

What You Should Know Before Buying a Home
League of Savings Associations
1709 New York Ave. NW
Washington, D.C. 20006

The Confusing World of Health Foods
(Publication 79-2108)
Dept. of Health and Human Services/Food and Drug Administration
Consumers Communications
HFJ-10
5600 Fishers Lane
Rockville, MD 20857

Tips on Buying a Home
(Publication 24-154)
Better Business Bureau
1150 17th St. NW
Washington, D.C. 20036

Wise Home Buying
(Publication HUD-401)
Dept. of Housing and Urban Development
Public Service Center
451 7th St. SW
Washington, D.C. 20410

Before Buying Land . . . Get the Facts
(Publication HUD-183-1(8))
Dept. of Housing and Urban Development
Public Service Center
451 7th St. SW
Washington, D.C. 20410

Read Your Lease Between the "Lines"
(Pamphlet, 1979)
Public Interest Group of Michigan
Michigan Public Interest Research Group
Michigan State University
22 Student Services
East Lansing, MI 48824

Wise Rental Practices
(Publication HUD-470-NVACP)
Dept. of Housing and Urban Development
Public Service Center
451 7th St. SW
Washington, D.C. 20410

Tips on Renting an Apartment
(Publication 24146)
Better Business Bureau
1150 17th St. NW
Washington, D.C. 20036

Buying a Home? Don't Forget Those Closing Costs!
(Publication HUD-342-F(7))
Dept. of Housing and Urban Development
Public Service Center
451 7th St. SW
Washington, D.C. 20410

Low Cost, No Cost
(Pamphlet 1980)
Dept. of Energy
Public Affairs Office
Room 1E218 Forrestal Building
Washington, D.C. 20585

Tips for Energy Savers
(Publication DOE/OPA-0037)
Dept. of Energy
Public Affairs Office
Room 1E218 Forrestal Building
Washington, D.C. 20585

Be an Energy Miser in Your Home
(Publication HUD-324-PA(2))
Dept. of Housing and Urban Development
Public Service Center
451 7th St. SW
Washington, D.C. 20410

Tips on Saving Energy
(Publication 311-02217)
Better Business Bureau
1150 17th St. NW
Washington, D.C. 20036

1984 Gas Mileage Guide
(Publication DOE/CS-0024/11)
Dept. of Energy/Environmental Protection Agency
Public Affairs Office of Publications
Washington, D.C. 20460

How to Save Gasoline and Money
(Publication DOE/OPA-0044, 1979)
Dept. of Energy
Public Affairs Office
Room 1E218 Forrestal Building
Washington, D.C. 20585

Six Ways to Save Money on Your Utility Bills
(Pamphlet, 1977)
American Public Power Association
2600 Virginia Ave. NW
Washington, D.C. 20037

Your Social Security
(Publication HEW (SSA) 78-10035)
Dept. of Health and Human Services/Social Security Administration
1515 Broadway
New York, NY

Thinking About Retiring?
(Publication HEW (SSA) 79-10055)
Dept. of Health and Human Services/Social Security Administration
1515 Broadway
New York, NY

Tips and Refunds and Exchanges
(Publication 02207)
Better Business Bureau
1150 17th St. NW
Washington, D.C. 20036

Warranties: There Ought to Be a Law . . . There Is
Federal Trade Commission
Legal and Public Record
Room 130
Sixth and Pennsylvania Ave. NW
Washington, D.C. 20580

Tips on Guarantees and Warranties
(Publication 01248)
Better Business Bureau
1150 17th St. NW
Washington, D.C. 20036

Tips on Sales Contracts
(Publication 02208)
Better Business Bureau
1150 17th St. NW
Washington, D.C. 20036

Tips on Mail Order Shade Trees
(Publication 01286)
Better Business Bureau
1150 17th St. NW
Washington, D.C. 20036

Shopping by Mail
Federal Trade Commission
Legal and Public Record
Room 130
Sixth and Pennsylvania Ave. NW
Washington, D.C. 20580

Minimizing Mail Order Hassles
(Fact Sheet)
United Auto Workers Consumers Affairs Dept.
8000 E. Jefferson Ave.
Detroit, MI 48214

Know Your Rights Under the Fair Credit Reporting Act
(Pamphlet)
Federal Trade Commission
Legal and Public Record
Room 130
Sixth and Pennsylvania Ave. NW
Washington, D.C. 20580

If You Use a Credit Card
(Pamphlet, 1979)
Federal Reserve System
Division of Consumer Affairs
Washington, D.C. 20551

Questions and Answers Concerning Your Insured Savings
(12 pages, 1974)
Federal Home Loan Bank Board
Communications Office
Washington, D.C. 20552

The Language of Investing
(37 pages, 1978)
Merrill Lynch Pierce Fenner and Smith
1100 Connecticut Ave. NW
Suite 340
Washington, D.C. 20036

Investigate Before You Invest
(Publication SEC, 1968)
Securities and Exchange Commission
Office of Consumer Affairs
500 N. Capitol St. NW
Washington, D.C. 20549

How to Invest
(23 pages, 1980)
Standard and Poor's Corporation
25 Broadway
New York, NY 10004

People Power: What Communities Are Doing to Counter Inflation
(411 pages, 1980)
Office of Consumer Affairs
The White House
1600 Pennsylvania Ave. NW
Washington, D.C. 20500

Everybody's Money—A Family Financial Guide
(Magazine, Special issue 5, 1977)
Credit Union National Association
PO Box 431
Madison, WI 53701

Plain Talk About IRAs
(Publication 1-15-1)

Federal Trade Commission
Legal and Public Record
Room 130
Sixth and Pennsylvania Ave. NW
Washington, D.C. 20580

A Primer on Medicines
(Publication (FDA) 79-3079)
Dept. of Health and Human Services/Food and Drug Administration
Consumers Communications
HFJ-10
5600 Fishers Lane
Rockville, MD 20857

Generic Drugs Save $$$
(Pamphlet, 1978)
Washington Public Interest Research Group
Student Union Bldg., FK-10
University of Washington
Seattle, WA 98195

The Big Quack Attack: Medical Devices
(Publication HEW (FDA) 80-4022)
Dept. of Health and Human Services/Food and Drug Administration
Consumers Communications
HFJ-10
5600 Fishers Lane
Rockville, MD 20857

Hocus-Pocus as Applied to Arthritis
(Publication HEW (FDA) 81-1080)
Dept. of Health and Human Services/Food and Drug Administration
Consumers Communications
HFJ-10
5600 Fishers Lane
Rockville, MD 20857

How to Shop for Health Insurance
(Publication 582G)
Consumer Information Center
Public Documents Distribution Center
Pueblo, CO 81009

Facts About Health Insurance
(Publication 03238)
Better Business Bureau
1150 17th St. NW
Washington, D.C. 20036

Your Medicare Handbook
(Publication (SSA) 79-10050)
Dept. of Health and Human Services/Social Security Administration
Call or write your local office

A Brief Explanation of Medicare
(Publication (SSA) 79-10043)
Dept. of Health and Human Services/Social Security Administration
Call or write your local office

If You Become Disabled
(Publication HEW (SSA) 79-10029)
Dept. of Health and Human Services/Social Security Administration
Call or write your local office

Cancer Quackery: Past and Present
(Publication HEW (FDA) 77-3039)
Dept. of Health and Human Services/Food and Drug Administration
Consumers Communications
HFJ-10
5600 Fishers Lane
Rockville, MD 20857

How to Select a Nursing Home
(5 pages, 1979)
United Neighbors in Action
491 65th St.
Oakland, CA 94609

A Consumer's Guide to the Federal Trade Commission
(46 pages, 1977)
Paul H. Douglas Consumer Research Center
1012 14th St. NW
Room 901
Washington, D.C. 20005

How to Complain and Get Results
(Fact Sheet)
Federal Trade Commission

Legal and Public Record
Room 130
Sixth and Pennsylvania Ave. NW
Washington, D.C. 20580

Consumer Information Catalogue
Consumer Information Center
Public Documents Distribution Center
Pueblo, CO 81009

The Consumer and the Small Claims Court
(4 pages, 1978)
California State Dept. of Consumer Affairs
1020 N. St.
Sacramento, CA 95814

Fraud and Deception
United Auto Workers Consumers Affairs Department
8000 E. Jefferson Ave.
Detroit, MI 48214

SOURCES AND RESOURCES

This book is the beginning, I trust, of a lifelong journey. Once you discover how much fun it is to add $5,000.00 or $10,000.00 to the money that you get back from Uncle Sam . . . once you see the sheer joy of watching your stock zoom from 4 to 400 . . . or the almost erotic euphoria of counting your gold coins, fingering your priceless collection of rare stamps, polishing your diamonds . . . once these pleasures have become commonplace, you will be hooked.

This book has served as an introduction to the world of investments and personal savings. But you may ask, where do you go from here? What magazines, journals, and additional financial investment books can help you on the path to investment success? I would suggest that you start with the financial pages of a good newspaper. Study the daily give and take of stocks, bonds and other forms of collateral. You'll learn a great deal, and such study can be as fascinating as watching the World Series. I would also suggest that you read several annual reports put out by some of the major and smaller corporations—several dozen if you can. Again, a great deal about how a company is doing can be gleaned from this source, and most companies are delighted to send them to you. Send away for as much free information as possible, as a rule. You'd be surprised at how much of it can be helpful in familiarizing yourself with the investment world. One word of warning: you're going to be flooded by phone calls from hotshot salesmen promising the world. Listen to every word, but don't buy a thing. Remember, you're doing this for educational purposes.

Next, I would suggest getting ahold of a few copies of some of the financial magazines, such as *Money, Fortune, Forbes,* and *Business.* (Don't subscribe first. If necessary, spend a few hours at the library reviewing them. See which magazines look appealing, which provide you with the most information for your needs. Then subscribe if you wish.)

Finally, read some of the more specialized finance and investment books. I would recommend almost anything by Sylvia Porter. She's the grand lady of finance—I wish everyone could write as well as she. A couple of other particularly good books are *The New York Times Book of Money,* and Jane Bryant Quinn's *Book of Money*. There are always new books on how to make a fortune, and many of them can be quite helpful. One final tip—perhaps the best finance books of all are the amazing documents put out by the I.R.S. And most delightful of all, they are free.